BEGOSO CABIN

9-4-2000

Happy Mona!
Birthday Mona!
I Treasure our
friendship.

Love,
La Merle

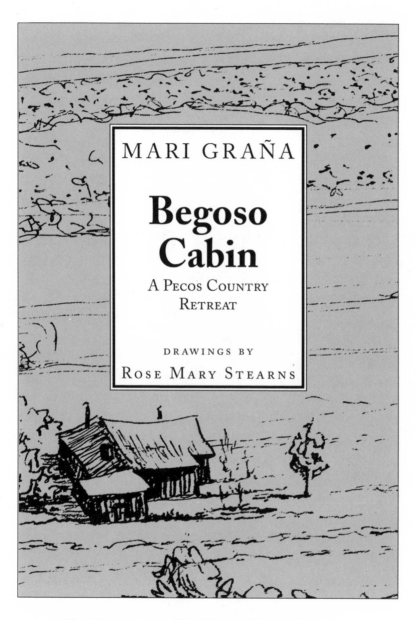

MARI GRAÑA

Begoso Cabin

A Pecos Country
Retreat

DRAWINGS BY
ROSE MARY STEARNS

THE UNIVERSITY OF NEW MEXICO PRESS *Albuquerque*

Library of Congress Cataloging-in-Publication Data
Graña, Mari, 1936–
Begoso cabin / Mari Graña ; drawings by Rose Mary Stearns. — 1st ed. p. cm.
ISBN 0-8263-2098-8
Includes bibliographical references (p. 153).   1. Hispanic Americans—Pecos River Region
(N.M. and Tex.)—Social life and customs.   2. Graña, Mari, 1936–   3. Pecos River
Region (N.M. and Tex.)—Social life and customs.   4. Pecos River Region (N.M. and
Tex.)—Biography.   I. Title.
F802.P3 G7 1999
305.868'07649—dc21

Designed by: LiMiTeD Edition Book Design, Linda Mae Tratechaud

For Cor, vanquisher of vipers

*Tell me the landscape in which you live,
and I will tell you who you are.*

José Ortega y Gasset

Begoso Cabin

PART

Discovery

ONE

1

Spring has not yet reached this high into the mountains of northern New Mexico, but the April sun is already here. The late afternoon air is warm as I walk the half mile along the dry wagon road that leads to the ranch gate. The road cuts through the still winter-dead meadow that stretches out beyond the gate, a mile or more east from my cabin. Anu, my brown Labrador pup, scampers along behind me, his nose to the dirt. Now and then he stops, head cocked, ears full forward, sniffs, then pounces on a fat black beetle unlucky enough to pick this moment to cross the road.

The late-season snow last weekend was so heavy that some of the branches on the juniper trees at the meadow edge are broken. But there is no sign of dampness now on the dusty red earth. Only in the thick dark sand, where one of my neighbor's cows broke through under the barbed wire fence where it straddles a side channel leading down to the dry bed of Begoso Creek and sank her imprint. Water has oozed up into the deep hoofmark, seeking a new surface, as if rising in a well. The sunlight is at a deep slant, already casting the toe of Rowe Mesa into shadow. When I reach the heavy chain-link gate, I turn and cross through the meadow along the fence posts and climb down the low bank to return to the cabin along the creek bottom.

Multiple rows of tiny tracks are fresh in the dry sand, all headed upstream in parallel. I must have just missed the afternoon rabbit race. A larger set of tracks runs with them. These are probably coyote, but he was there before the rabbits; the wind has blown his trace to the edges of recognition. At the junction of a narrow arroyo that drains into the Begoso off the ridge to the south, a set of bear tracks enters the creek bed and, after a short distance, disappears up into the meadow. I walk always with an eye out for snakes, a vigilance that is the price of this solitude.

The clouded sky does not portend rain: tomorrow will be a beauty. Along my way an occasional young cottonwood reaches its bare arms to the afternoon sun. The creek banks are lined with a thick residue of broken branches woven with dead grass and glued with mud—a sign that not long before the Begoso has flooded two to three feet high with runoff brought down the canyon from the hundreds of gullies that drain the melting winter. It seems inconceivable that this even, sandy pathway on which I am walking leads a secret life as a torrent.

I follow the creek upstream to where it curves in close to the cabin. Anu is frisking and sniffing and chomping on sticks and occasionally collapsing onto his bottom to chew out from between his toes a cholla thorn that has blown into the creek bed from the meadow. Sometimes I need to help him; his four-month-old paws have not yet hardened to this rough land.

ↄჳ

The stone cabin faces east like a Navajo hogan. In the cold sunrise, a cacophony of coyotes celebrates matins on the south ridge that shoulders the vertical, orange, tree-dotted cliffs of Rowe Mesa. In the distance, far beyond the meadow, the wall of Bernal Mesa rises into the morning above the Pecos River. The day will indeed be the beauty I saw coming on our walk last evening, but the sun is still too low for warmth. Anu sits in the open doorway, shivering with excitement at the yelping coming from the ridge. For Anu, every day of his new life presents wondrous revelations: some are exciting, like the coyote song he is listening to; some questionable, like the beetles in the road on our walk; some fearsome, like the bailing-wire handle to Andelecio's woodbox that clamped down on his neck one day last week when Andy and I were having a cup of coffee in his house in Ribera. The woodbox came out from behind the big iron stove tight around Anu's neck, he screaming his high-squeal puppy yelp at the monster that was holding him fast, creating indulgent entertainment for his audience.

The morning wind has not yet settled into its steady daytime draw up Begoso Canyon, and the smoke from the firepit in front of the cabin circles in all directions. It swirls into my face, flapping the pages of my notebook and teasing my nostrils with the sweet pungency of piñon, then moves on in its circular quest for direction. Anu has now dug himself a nest in the dirt at the side of the firepit and is curled in restless readiness, watching a magpie who returns his vigil from a fence stake a few feet away. The magpie sits black like a crow, facing us on the fence, squawking at us with defiant caws, and then, like a flasher, flips his white at us as he flies to find a better vantage point. I leave my coffee warming on the grill over the firepit and go into the cabin to search for the granola I forgot to bring from town. Instead, my breakfast will be rice with powdered milk and sugar. Forgot the raisins too.

☙

Begoso cabin lies in a wide canyon at the edge of Begoso Creek some four miles west of the Pecos River and State Highway 3, which runs along its banks. Forty miles east of Santa Fe and twenty miles west of Las Vegas, New Mexico, the highway leaves the interstate that connects New Mexico with Colorado and states north, and winds through a series of villages—Ribera, San Miguel, El Pueblo, Sena, Villanueva. Beyond Villanueva, the highway climbs up out of the river valley and runs in almost a straight line through miles of sparsely settled ranch lands, finally connecting with U.S. 40, the major cross-country interstate. The villages along the river were once part of the San Miguel del Bado land grant, given to area settlers by King Carlos IV of Spain. Today, the main villages are San Miguel and Villanueva, for these are where the two parish churches are located, and Ribera, a half mile from San Miguel, which has the post office.

The closest village to my cabin is El Pueblo, where the dirt wagon road up Begoso Canyon begins. El Pueblo is named for the remains of an early pueblo settlement inhabited by Pecos Indians, probably as a summer camp, before the coming of the Spanish to settle New Mexico in the late sixteenth century. The villages are still largely Hispanic, although in recent years a few Anglos have moved into areas along the river. Although today the people are bilingual, Spanish—or the New Mexican version of Spanish—is still the language of neighborliness and village commerce.

The dirt wagon road to my cabin has wound through Begoso Canyon for at least the past two hundred years, perhaps longer. The grant settlers used it to get firewood and flagstone for building their houses, and for access to the backlands for sheep and cattle grazing. A mile beyond my cabin, the dirt road leaves the canyon and climbs steeply up the ridge to the north, giving access to a couple of remote ranches miles farther along. The road is barely passable on this ascent, full of rocks and gullies that deepen after every storm. It is an alternative route to the ranches and seldom used. Few people pass by my cabin, only a couple of neighbors who have grazing lands in the canyon beyond me, and these maybe only once or twice a month.

Soon after I moved into the cabin, I went exploring up the canyon beyond where the road starts up the ridge. The steep walls quickly narrowed around me, and the dense vegetation of willow and scrub oak, chokecherry and chamisa soon stopped me from reaching the top, where the creek works its way down from Rowe Mesa above. I would need a machete to cut my way through. This must be why the creek got the name "Begoso," which in Spanish means "covered with vegetation."

2

Finding the Begoso cabin was pure chance. I had been searching for such a place ever since I had moved to Santa Fe five years before. Almost every Sunday I would take the real estate section of the Santa Fe paper, get in my pickup, and check out the land sales. I explored all over northern New Mexico. I tramped over miles of acreage, crawling under cattle gates, ignoring No Trespassing signs. I looked at land with houses on it and land without. And I didn't just stick to the advertised land. I thought that if I found the perfect spot, perhaps the owner would decide that, just maybe, it might be for sale. But for all my explorations, I couldn't find the right place. The land I looked at was either too expensive, or too large, or didn't have enough trees, or was too steep, or too close to a neighbor, or too close to town. If there was a highway in sight from anywhere on the property, I scratched it off immediately.

Then one day last summer I saw advertised a large piece of land at an extremely low price. There was a number for the realtor listing this parcel, and I called. As I suspected from the price, there was a hang-up. The land belonged to an estate trust back East. The title wasn't clear, and the owners had put a low price on the land hoping that a new owner would straighten out the problem and get the place out of their hair.

I had learned enough about land hassles in New Mexico to avoid a title problem, no matter what the price: the people here are still arguing over pre-1848 Spanish and Mexican land grants. I have a lawyer friend who went all the way to Spain, to the Archives of the Indies in Seville, to try to figure out who once owned what and hence who maybe now owns what. And then there are the parcels acquired through inheritance. These were seldom surveyed since it was all in the family anyway, and often no one knows for sure where the boundaries are. Fences tell you nothing. Before I would buy land in New Mexico, I would need a survey by a licensed civil engineer and a title insurance affidavit to go with it. I told all this to the realtor on the phone, and she laughed and told me I was approaching this thing correctly. Then she said she had another piece she was sure was all clear. Realtors always have a backup possibility in their hip pocket when you call. Having been disappointed so many times, I was skeptical. But I agreed to go with her the next day to look at it.

The realtor picked me up in a four-wheel-drive truck. We drove east of Santa Fe on the interstate for about forty miles, then turned south on the state road that follows along the Pecos River. The first village we came to was Ribera, where we crossed the AT&SF

railroad tracks and abruptly turned left onto a dirt lane. We pulled up shortly in front of a large adobe house. Andelecio, the owner of the land we had come to see, strode out the kitchen door and waved a greeting. He climbed into the truck with us and introduced himself to me as "Andy." He had grown up in Ribera, and the big adobe house where we picked him up had belonged to his parents. Andy and the realtor were old friends. She had been working with him for months making sure that the easement agreements on the dirt road and the property boundaries were all in order.

The next village downriver was San Miguel. There was an open area in the center of the village that looked like it had once been a plaza; now the state highway crosses through the middle of it. The area was dotted with crumbling ruins, with newer buildings in among them. The whole was dominated by a hulking old church with a historical marker in front of it. "That's the church the original settlers built in the early nineteenth century," Andy said as we drove on. "And across the road you can see where the tracks of the Santa Fe Trail crossed the river and came up into the plaza." I caught a brief glimpse of two wagon ruts disappearing into the trees toward the river.

We continued south along the river for about five miles till we came to the village of El Pueblo. This village divides into two clusters of settlement: Upper Pueblo contains a few old adobes as well as some newer houses and a few mobile homes. There is a cemetery and a little pink church with a tin roof. There is also a tiny adobe building at the edge of the road. As we drove by, I saw a sign that said Closed on the rickety-looking door. I asked Andy what the old building was used for. "That's the store for these parts," Andy laughed, "although there's nothing in there but some soft drinks and a few old candy bars. The proprietor lives across the road and occasionally comes over to open the door." Lower Pueblo looked like it had more activity, largely because of a long building with neon beer signs in the windows and three gas pumps in the front. A row of pickup trucks lined the establishment.

Just beyond the bar, we turned west onto a dirt wagon road, barred by a locked gate. Andy got out, unlocked the gate, and waited until we drove through to lock it. After we had bounced over four miles of barely passable muddy ruts—it had rained recently and there were huge puddles in the road—and Andy had opened and closed five cattle gates, I saw over a rise in a meadow a little stone cabin far in the distance. I knew immediately it was what I had been looking for. It was the Begoso cabin. The landscape of the canyon—the rocky pine-covered ridges, the long wide meadow with the escarpment of Rowe Mesa rising in the background—suddenly became the place I had dreamed about.

We drove up to the cabin. Andy opened the old wrought-iron bedstead that served as a gate to the *portal*, the roof-covered porch at the front of the cabin, and unlocked the padlocks on the old plank doors. Inside, the rooms were covered with pack rat nests in among a scattering of rough, broken-down pieces of furniture. Some shelves, a table, a rickety cot, an old chair with the springs poking through. The mud-plaster of the walls had dribbled all over the stone floors, probably from leaks in the tin roof. The windows were boarded over, the glass in shards on the mudded floor. In a corner of one of the rooms was a hole to the outside that the rats must be using to bring in their possessions. Behind where a woodstove had once stood, oilcloth was peeling off the kitchen wall. The place smelled of musty dirt and rat droppings. No one had lived in here for years. I immediately saw beyond the rat nests and broken windows and melting walls to what the cabin had once been, and what it could again become.

We went out to the storeroom. "Watch out for rattlers in here," Andy said as he unlocked the door.

"What do you do about the rattlers?" I asked, probably sounding rather naive.

"Shoot 'em," he said. Since we didn't have a gun with us, I didn't think that was enough of an answer. But if there were any snakes under the two-foot floor-covering of rat nests, they didn't show themselves.

"Let's go look at the land," Andy said to me, after I had gingerly poked my nose through the doorway of the storeroom and promptly removed it again.

We climbed up the steep rocky north ridge through the piñon-juniper forest until we stood on an outcrop high enough that we could see over the trees and down into the meadow. The wind was fresh in the trees and the tall grass in the meadow far below us was rippling like the backs of a herd of running horses. We followed the fenceline east along the ridge to the end of the property and then scrambled back down to the road where the realtor was waiting to pick us up.

As we bumped back along the dirt road, Andy told me about the old man who had built the cabin and about the people who owned property along the way. They are all Hispanos, as is Andelecio, and most of them are descendants of the families who settled here a couple hundred years ago.

We left Andy off at his house, and I told him I would "think about it." No doubt he could tell I was completely enchanted, but one doesn't want to sound overly eager. Driving back to Santa Fe with the realtor, I found it hard to keep up a conversation. I was still stunned by the beauty of what I had just seen.

For the next few weeks I agonized over what to do. The price was fair enough, but I had been thinking in terms of maybe 40 acres. The 240 acres that surround the cabin was more land than I had ever dreamed of buying, and therefore more expensive than I thought I could afford. On the other hand, having that much land around me would protect me from any encroachments that might occur over the years. And the reason I wanted to buy land in the first place was to be able to withdraw from the world whenever I wished. There has always been something of the hermit in me, and beyond the beauty of the land and the charm of the little stone cabin, the remoteness of the canyon was exactly what I was looking for. I considered for a moment the financially reasonable thought that I might share the cabin and the land with a friend but immediately gave up the idea. It would take all the retirement money I had been carefully hoarding for some unpredictable future, but the place would have to be all mine or I wouldn't have it at all.

Perhaps there was something more at work in me than worry about money. A dream is a dream. And there is something frightening about a dream turning into a possibility. If I were to buy the land, I would have to face the prospect that it wouldn't be a dream any more. In some strange way there is a loss here. And the disquieting realization that I would have to live up to my own commitment to myself. It takes time to work this through, to weigh the options, to consider that there might someday be another dream, but if all the money were gone, it would never happen.

And then there was the area itself. Would I get along with my neighbors? Would they accept an Anglo woman living alone in the wilds of Begoso Canyon? I had heard stories of Hispanic resentment toward Anglos moving into their territory. Driving back along the road from the cabin, Andy had talked about the people living in the river villages. He had laughingly said that there were family feuds in the villages that would make the fights of the Hatfields and McCoys seem like a tea party. Would I be drawn into something like that?

My realtor kept calling but finally gave up on me. She moved away, but I don't think that was because of my procrastinations. Several weeks went by. I was still mulling: afraid to make a move; fearful the cabin would be sold. Another realtor took over, this one a good friend of many years. She knows me well enough to know that Begoso Canyon was the place. She warned me that she was getting phone calls and would have to start returning them if I didn't get moving. I went out with her to look again at the land. It was even more beautiful than I had remembered. It was already September now. The summer rains had turned the meadow an intense green, filling it with yellow black-eyed susans, wild coreopsis, and pale purple Michaelmas daisies. Along Begoso Creek, the cottonwoods were thinking about turning and the chamisa lining the banks was topped with golden crowns. It would take all my money. I made the offer.

However, even in the passion of making a dream decision, I wasn't taking anyone's word that everything was legally clear. All my savings were tied up in this decision. I insisted on a survey and title insurance, and threw a few other things into the deal like cleaning the pack rats out of the cabin and getting the well pump working. Sure enough there was trouble, but it was still Andy's trouble. It took months to work out the knots, but finally, in early January, the papers were signed and recorded with the San Miguel county clerk. The Begoso cabin was mine.

3

Natividad Ortiz, who built my cabin, settled this land with his parents and brothers and sisters sometime around the turn of the century. The Ortiz family was not originally from the river villages. According to one of my neighbors, the family moved into Begoso Canyon from Cañón del Pueblo up on Rowe Mesa. Water was scarce on the mesa, and Begoso Canyon offered a better water source as well as good pasture land. In 1911, after the U.S. government opened the land for homesteading, Natividad filed his claim for the cabin and surrounding 160 acres.

There were several children in the Ortiz family, and the youngest, Blasita, was born in the cabin. It is difficult to even imagine the hardship of living with little children in the two small rooms that made up this cabin. When Blasita was two, however, the family moved to irrigated land down by the Pecos River and settled in the village at El Pueblo. But Natividad remained. He lived out here, raising sheep and dry crops, until he met Clotilda. She apparently preferred village life, so he, too, moved to El Pueblo. Natividad's marriage to Clotilda was short and tragic. Clotilda died very young, and their little daughter, Rafaelita, died soon after her mother. An elderly woman in the village told me that Natividad was so despondent at the loss of his wife and daughter that he returned to live as a hermit out here in the Begoso cabin until the years of the Great Depression. Finally, economic hardship drove him to seek work, sheepherding, in Nevada. In his absence, the cabin was used for periods by family members, raising food and keeping some animals on the land until Natividad returned in the late 1950s to spend his last years here. He died in 1967. Since then the cabin had stood empty, used perhaps a couple of times a year as a shelter for hunters, until I purchased it from Andelecio.

I haven't yet found anyone in the village who knows exactly when the cabin was built. The package of papers I received from Andy when we closed the deal includes the homestead deed to Natividad Ortiz, 160 acres in the Territory of New Mexico. It is dated 1911, the year before New Mexico became a state, and signed by M. P. LeRoy, secretary to Pres. William H. Taft. I'm told that even before Natividad claimed the land, a rough house had been built by his family, but aside from a couple of old juniper posts sticking out of the ground over by the sheep corral, there is no sign of this first structure.

Sometime later Natividad and his family built the first two rooms of the stone cabin. These are the kitchen and what is now my "dining room"—at least it holds a table on which to eat. The two rooms are connected by an inside door; one enters from the outside into the kitchen. The ceilings of these rooms are made of huge, flat pieces of stone set on top of the vigas, the horizontal supports for the ceilings. It must have taken the full complement of Ortiz brothers to help Natividad lift these slabs into place. It is uncommon to see stone ceilings, even in this part of the world. The weight must be tremendous, but the supporting vigas are solid pine logs. In 1937—the date is carved into the stone floor—a third, larger room was added. The addition is joined at an L to the original structure, and its door opens only to the outside. From the kitchen, one has to go out under the *portal,* the outside covered porch, to enter this room, now my bedroom. The ceiling is made of wide, rough-sawn planks, the bark still clinging to the edges, supported again by log vigas.

The interior walls of the cabin are mud-plastered, and the floors are broad, even flagstones. The stone walls are actually double—two separate parallel walls that leave a three-inch air pocket in between for insulation. Each of the three rooms has a single, foot-and-a-half square window with four tiny panes.

Next to the bedroom, at the end of the L, is the storage room. It has a stone base, about three feet in height, all around it. From there to the tin roof the walls are formed by narrow, vertical piñon logs, each one carefully squared off with an adze so the logs fit tightly together. The old roof is made of thick, corrugated tin that needs only occasional dabs of plastic roof cement to become impermeable again. Under the V of the roof above the three main rooms of the house—the storeroom has a separate, slanted shed roof—is an attic, now empty, with a small, padlocked door at each end. Natividad packed a six-inch layer of mud on the attic floor to keep the winter cold and the summer heat out of the rooms below. The roof extends out beyond the cabin wall to form the *portal*, which keeps the rain off as you walk from one room to the other.

To my humble eye, the stone cabin is a piece of art, constructed with amazing craftsmanship considering the tools Natividad worked with. But there is nothing decorative about it. It is as tight and functional and solid as one can make with an adze and a tree trunk, stones and mud. But Natividad let his fancy soar just a little on the doors. They are made of simple, planed planks held together on the inside by crosspieces, and they close on a high sill. He painted the doors white on the outside, and then carefully trimmed the white with blue edging around the top and bottom and sides, with a thick blue line across the center to give the illusion of paneling. I carefully scrubbed years of grime off them. The paint is greatly faded, but his faux paneling still works its effect.

Natividad was much shorter than I. I've been out here for several weeks now and I often still forget to step high and duck at the same time when I go in and out the doors. I usually wear my glasses on the top of my head when I'm not reading, and one day I smashed them on the low lintel of the doorway as I was coming out of the bedroom. Fortunately the glasses are of the variety you buy off a stand at the supermarket. I made a note on my grocery list to lay in a couple of extra pairs on my next trip to town.

After twenty-seven years of abandonment, there wasn't much left at the cabin to tell me about its former owner. But in addition to the talk of the few villagers who still remember the old man, I find my own clues to Natividad's life as I wander about the place. The crumbling walls of the sheep corral yielded the ornate headpiece of an old iron bed, the foot of which is leaning against the storeroom wall. The headpiece had been attached to two narrow logs to make a gate. I encountered it half buried under a chamisa bush, the rough hand-forged hinges still usable. Across the wagon road are the remains of a root cellar, the stone walls still standing, the log roof fallen into the pit. In the meadow not far from the root cellar is a circular floor, about fifteen feet in diameter, of large flat pieces of flagstone fitted tightly together. I asked Andelecio what this floor was used for. He replied that it was a *herra*—he didn't know a word for it in English—and said that it was used to thresh wheat and beans. A horse was led around the edge of the circle pulling a roller attached to a post in the center. As the horse walked, the roller shucked the beans and grain against the flat stones. My mind jumped back thirty years ago to when I lived in Andalusia. I had seen horses out in the fields walking in circles pulling the same sort of contraption. In Spain it was called an *arrastra*—a word that is not in my Spanish–English dictionary, although it probably derives from *arrastrar*, to haul or drag. Presumably the editor didn't

think anyone would need to know about such an archaic practice, or maybe he never heard of it himself, or maybe there just isn't an English translation.

According to my neighbors, Natividad raised corn and beans in the large meadow in front of the cabin and on the upper meadow to the south. His crops were watered only by the summer rains. There is now no sign of these meadows ever having been planted, and the junipers are starting to invade them again. More recently, when Andelecio took over the place, he ran cows in these meadows. The wiry high-desert grass is still cropped short, although not as short as the grass just beyond the barbed wire fence where my neighbor's cows have trimmed it to the dirt. Down by the well Natividad had planted a plum orchard, the trees now stunted and tangled from the unpruned shoots. Just beyond the abandoned orchard, a lone apple tree struggles to bud again in this cruelest month, its only companion—a peach—now dead.

Inside the cabin there were only a few scraps of furniture left. A couple of tables, a useless coil-sprung chair, and some rough benches. And Natividad's bed. I've been sleeping on his bed for too many nights now, and "original" as it may be, it will soon have to retire to the storeroom. Natividad was not only shorter than I, his back was certainly tougher than mine. The bed is a wooden frame, crossed by planks and covered with fine-mesh chicken wire. Even with the foam rubber pad I put over the wire and a down sleeping bag, I still can't sleep through the night on the thing. An old rough-plank doghouse was still standing under the *portal* by the kitchen door. I've recycled it as a table for the firepit. Anu doesn't need it; he sleeps with me on Natividad's bed.

In a stand of junipers down by the creek I found Natividad's garbage dump. An archaeologist would call this a kitchen midden.

And a kitchen midden is an archaeologist's paradise. From the tell-tale detritus of humankind the daily life of entire cultures can be pieced together. Disposing of garbage in any way other than as far as the arm can pitch it is no doubt an urban idea. But even in cities, the idea hasn't always yet taken hold. I am again reminded of the years I lived in Spain, of looking out the window of a modern apartment complex in Seville and seeing the bank of the Guadalquivir— the river that once delivered to the motherland the priceless plunder of a continent—littered with plastic bottles, tin cans, newspapers, old shoes and clothing, a toilet seat. All tossed from the windows of the new apartment buildings that turn their backs to the river.

My delight in discovering Natividad's garbage dump is no doubt akin to that of the archaeologist who uncovers the midden of some Iron Age habitation. And perhaps some of the old man's droppings are not that time-distant in content. In among the junk I found the remains of a pedal-powered grinding wheel. It took me a while to determine the purpose of this contraption, since the grinding stones have now disappeared, perhaps under the earth. The machine has a wooden seat, now only splinters, attached to a metal frame. You sit with your feet on the metal pedals that turn the rods that turn the stones that grind the knives, axes, chisels, sheep shears, or any other objects in need of a cutting edge.

Several old truck tires were scattered around the place, the smoothed surfaces now showing dirty white threads. And the tailgate of a Chevrolet—garbage, I suppose, of Natividad's later years, replacing the horse of his earlier life. His favorite lard brand was from the Sunshine Packing Company of Albuquerque, the red-painted label depicting a large happy pig munching a corncob. Pancakes and tortillas were a staple, according to the dusty drapery of masa and flour bags I found hanging from the viga nails along with the lard cans. Out behind the cabin I found the scoop of a shovel pounded out of a piece of metal. It has become my ash scoop for the stove and also doubles as a dust pan. Several washtubs dot the terrain—bottomless, eaten through by the dirt on which they died. From the main midden at the creek bank, I learned from the size of old shoes that Natividad was a small man; that he liked sardines a lot; that he preferred K-C Brand baking powder to make his biscuits; and—from the number of Arabs in long yellow cloaks raising cups to their lips—that Hills Bros. coffee was his favorite. Rust has robbed me of the name of his favorite beer, which he apparently drank often, and the labels of myriad bottles of spirits have long washed away. Natividad left me half a can of his pipe tobacco, George Washington brand, in a large, faded red, white, and blue tin container. I gave the tobacco to the wind and filled the tin with Anu's dog biscuits.

Nearly succumbing to the moral compulsion that grips the ecological consciousness of our late twentieth-century minds, I considered cleaning up the creek midden and the detritus scattered out around the cabin. Picking up all the rusted sardine cans, worn-out shoes, dirt-filled whiskey bottles, and bits and pieces of old metal and wire, packing it all into plastic trash bags and hauling it off to the San Miguel County dump. But then I thought better of it. Why should I pick up Natividad's droppings? Are they not as much a part of this wondrous landscape as the winter-dead chamisa crowns, the prickly pear and cholla in the meadow grass, the bear who left his tracks across Begoso Creek, Anu's black beetles, the coyotes singing their dawn-song? As the stones he broke from their outcrop to build his cabin, the same stones he used to build his sheep corral and to line the walls of his well? Last week I climbed to the top of the north ridge, to where the barbed wire fence divides my land from my neighbor's. I felt a flush of greedy excitement as I looked back down into the meadow, and then up to the shoulder of Rowe Mesa to the south—it was all mine!

And then I was ashamed. What arrogance! Of course it is not mine. My tenure on this land will be the briefest instant of its perennial existence. The next settler in the stone cabin will not be able to rummage through my garbage, because my life is not Natividad's. But I'll make sure he can read Natividad's life, for I will leave his trash heap just as it is. I'll bet the old man is giggling in his grave to think that someone is preserving his droppings!

4

I hired the Martinez brothers from the village, Presilino and Secundo, to help me fix up the place. They worked on the cabin every day for three weeks this February, snow permitting, and covered the mud interior with plaster mixed with the red sand from Begoso Creek. They replaced the dribbling mud mortar on the outer stone walls with cement and moved Natividad's old sagging outhouse from its location adjacent to the cabin to a more discreet distance behind a juniper tree. They hooked up new stovepipe for the old green-and-yellow enameled cookstove I found in a junk shop in Albuquerque and a new heatstove from the hardware store in Santa Fe.

"We need to burn off the dead meadow plants around the cabin to keep the snakes out," Presilino advised. "Don't worry, the grass will come back nice and green and low." And indeed little tufts of green are just beginning to push up through the blackened earth.

I was concerned that Anu be safe at night from the coyotes, so the brothers enclosed a large area for him with hog fencing in front of the cabin *portal.* For gate hinges we used the old forged iron ones from the bedstead gate in Natividad's stone sheep corral just beyond the cabin fence. Like the colosseum in Rome, which supplied the building materials for the medieval city, scarcely making a dent in the massive structure, the walls of Natividad's huge sheep corral provided the flagstones for the firepit, walkways to the fence gates, and a floor in front of the cabin on which to sit out of the meadow mud.

The door to the storeroom has a small square cut out at the bottom. This was for Natividad's fifteen to twenty cats to go in and out of the rain. He loved his animals. I'm told that he would drive his truck the sixty miles to Las Vegas and back just to buy his cats their favorite cat food. Inside the storeroom, rusty recycled lard cans, hanging from thick twenty-penny nails pounded into the vigas, were filled with bolts and screws, horseshoe nails, bits of wire and metal he was saving. The room still contained a few old tools, the foot of the iron bed—the headpiece to which he had used for his sheep gate—old pieces of tack, a dismantled animal trap, and his hat. Even though part of the brim is chewed away, providing bedding for some critter, I have left it hanging on the nail where he last put it. One morning when Presilino and Secundo were working in the storeroom, they discovered a stash of dynamite in a twenty-pound lard can that was hanging from a nail next to the hat. Somehow over the years the decomposing dynamite had not exploded and blown the cabin clear to Las Vegas. Presilino gingerly took the lard can off the nail and let the wind take the deadly powder out into the meadow.

Presilino brought me a gift for my new home, a picture of La Conquistadora. She is the statue of the Virgin that Fray Alonso de

Benavides brought to Santa Fe in 1626. Don Diego de Vargas brought her back to Santa Fe after he recaptured the city in 1692. An Indian revolt had driven the Spanish, along with their statue, out of New Mexico twelve years earlier. La Conquistadora lives now in the ca- thedral, where she presides as the *patrona* of the city. I found an old Mexican tin frame that just fits the picture. She is watching over me now from the wall as I write at Natividad's table.

The Brothers Martinez finished the repair work on the house a month ago. Over the past weekends, except for the last when the snow made the road impassable, I have loaded up my pickup in Santa Fe and hauled out here the minimal furniture I need. Some chairs to set around Natividad's table; an old pie safe that I found in a secondhand store in Las Vegas; a couple of metal chairs, found one day in the Santa Fe dump, to set out by the firepit—the plastic covering the metal tubing is shot, but the chairs are still sturdy. I brought out some extra pots and pans from my Santa Fe house and clothes to keep in the chest of drawers I got at the flea market, which also provided a washstand with a mirrored cabinet above it. The pièce de résistance is my grandmother's Victorian wood rocking chair, an exceedingly ugly piece of furniture that spent its more recent years relegated to the basement. Until now. It is just the thing for rocking and reading in front of the bedroom stove.

The walls of the "dining room" are lined with sets of metal shelves from the hardware store, the kind that come in a box with all the requisite bolts and pieces and assembly directions. It took the better part of a day to figure out where all the bolts were supposed to go and how to put them together so they wouldn't wobble. But now they stand fourfold against the wall, firm and unwobbly, their shelves lined with canned chili and overcooked vegetables, mouse-proof plastic tubs and glass jars of dry goods, beer for the neighbors, gas cans and candles and kerosene lamps. I also bought a gas lantern; it was expensive, and I find I don't use it. Its rude humming glare exposes every corner of the room. I prefer the silent glow of the kerosene lamps. The light is soft and molds delicious shadows on the deep red of the river sand on the walls.

Since my cabin has no electricity or running water, I'm required to rethink the economies of daily life: the economy of daylight—structuring one's day in the cycle of the sun; the economy of heat—minimizing the hassle of chopping stove wood; the economy of water—minimizing the number of trips down to the well to haul back another heavy bucket. Anu is a great help in my water economy. So much water that would normally go down a sink drain—the water in which I boil spaghetti, the liquid from a can of string beans—here at the cabin all goes into his drinking bowl. And he laps it up with gusto. At the ecology store in Santa Fe I found a special kind of dishwashing soap. The label asserts it is not only harmless to plants, it actually breaks down into something they thrive on. So my dishwater feeds the chokecherry hedge I just planted and saves me an extra trip to the well. I once read that public utility planners assume the average U.S. household needs 250 gallons of water per day for domestic use. What a conservation program could be instantly implemented if the water lines ran only to the lot edge, and the average American had to carry his water in a bucket to the kitchen.

I brought some plastic construction buckets out from town. These are much lighter for hauling water than the heavy metal ones like those I found lying around the cabin, surviving Natividad, but now useless from rusted-out holes. The Coleman Company has made heating morning coffee and instant oatmeal far easier and faster than firing up the wood cookstove, except on those early mornings this winter when the heavy iron stove's main function was to heat the cold stone cabin walls. And there are other things that give me a leg up on Natividad: vacuum bottles are great for holding coffee hot through the day; Teflon-coated pots make dishwashing a snap; and my down sleeping bag must surely be cozier than a blanket roll. And of course I won't be getting up at dawn to tend the sheep he kept in the now-dilapidated stone corral or hoe the beans he planted on the meadows.

Lacking a refrigerator, I use the well to keep things cold. I found an old metal egg basket that will hold beer and soft drinks, and butter and bacon in zip-lock bags, and I submerge it in the water. But most of my food is canned or dry. Tubers will keep, as will apples for a time, and when summer comes I hope to get garlic and onions from the earth. I will plant apple trees this summer, and in a few years I will have more fruit than can be turned into jam from the chokecherry hedge. Then I will have to find out how to make the delicious fruit brandy I've tasted in the village. But I won't put in a vegetable garden, at least not now. I don't mind hauling the water up the slope from the well, but I don't want to be tied to the daily care of a garden. Then my cabin won't be a place of freedom, a place to come whenever I wish — and not when I don't.

In my Toyota four-wheel-drive pickup, I can traverse the four miles of wagon road to the village in half an hour — even counting the time it takes to open each of the five cattle gates, drive through, and close them again so the cows won't get mixed. Early on, Natividad made the trip by horse, and it must have taken a full day to do his errands in the village and ride back. Perhaps he stopped to visit his brothers and sisters in the long L-shaped adobe by the Pueblo gate, but rumor has it the Ortiz family didn't get on very well.

I don't have the papers that tell me when Natividad added an eighty-acre parcel to his original homestead tract, but he sold this piece to Andelecio in 1966. He scrawled his name illegibly on the deed and then made an *X*, his mark acknowledged by three witnesses. Then, in 1967, the old man died. This I know from the calendar still hanging on the wall in the kitchen. It was issued by Saibe's Confectionery, Medicinas Caseras. Eusebio Seguro, Prop. 144 Bridge St., Las Vegas, N. Mex., and shows a picture of Jesus, a brilliant light radiating from his body, appearing to a kneeling Mary Magdalene before an empty tomb. Below this scene, all the months have been torn off down to August. Some say he was ninety, some say less. On one of my trips to the village I stopped by the *camposanto*, the old cemetery in El Pueblo, to see if I could find him. In among a population of cement angels holding faded plastic flowers and watchful Madonnas—one of whom lives in a *nicho* made from an upended bathtub—I came upon a lone rusted metal marker poked into the ground. I was barely able to make out the words: Natividad Ortiz. Died August 25, 1967. Age 83 years, 7 months, 29 days. Natividad probably wouldn't have wanted an angel anyway.

The homestead passed to his sister Blasita, who lived in the rambling Ortiz adobe in Lower Pueblo where the road to Villanueva forks and a graveled road winds up onto the mesa, past the volunteer fire department and the new elementary–middle school, to Gonzales Ranch. Andelecio bought the property from Blasita a few years before she died. He ran cows on the meadows until he put the land up for sale. But the cabin was left to the pickings of hunters and field mice, and to drool its mud mortar to the snows and rain.

C

It is late afternoon; the wind that has blown steadily in Begoso Canyon all through the day has finally died. I have been sitting here in front of the firepit writing in my notebook since morning. The cold shadow of the cabin has captured me, but as I look out to the still-sunny meadow, I see the junipers at its edge shining in the electric air. The sun is giving each tree a sparkling individuality; they have lost for the moment their relationship as a forest. I have seen this intense light of New Mexico before in southern countries—Spain, Italy, North Africa; it is uncommon this far north in America. It is a stark, eerie, almost unreal brightness, like the moment after you rub your eyes and then open them again on a suddenly dazzling world. Like all magic moments, it passes quickly.

The red stones of the sheep corral are caught, too, in this brilliance. Each one is articulated by fine shadows. Each one shouts for attention: "Look at me! I'm not just part of a wall; I was set here for you to see me!" As if some unearthly hand had set each above and below and beside the others, placed separately, in some unfathomable design. As I watch, the shadows of the nearby trees lengthen until they touch the corral. The stones become a wall again, their moment of solitary transfiguration ended.

I remember having to read Henry Thoreau's *Walden* in high school. I grumbled with my classmates at the assignment, but deep down I was hooked. I wished someday there would be a pond in my life. I would sit day after day at the edge of it, like Thoreau, and wonder at the minutiae of nature. Later, other books like Aldo Leopold's *Sand County Almanac* and Annie Dillard's *Pilgrim at Tinker Creek* captured me. There is no pond here on Natividad's land, and the mighty Begoso flows only in the flash of a summer thunderstorm or as it carries the winter melt. The wildlife of the dry creek bed is only hinted at in the tracks left by a rabbit or the slither marks of a snake. The villagers tell me there are elk and bear and mountain lion on the walls of Rowe Mesa, but it is unlikely these wary creatures will let me see them. Only the occasional scat or a wind-blown track suggests the villagers may be right. There are no tadpoles or frogs or fish flashing in the ripple of gentle rapids as these writers tell about. But there are birds: lazy, gliding hawks—one flew over my head last week dangling a still-squirming lizard; Anu's morning magpie; owls that spook through the night; and a Rocky Mountain bluebird I saw the other day on a juniper near the fence. He was iridescent with a blueness brighter than any I have ever seen. I will have to add a birds-of-New-Mexico book to my shopping list. And there are eagles, though I haven't yet seen one. The villagers say they circle above the Nido del Aguila, the highest point I can see along the south wall of Rowe Mesa. A rabbit scampered across my path this morning between the outhouse and the stone corral, and Anu presented me with a dead field mouse when we went down to the well later. For a couple of days I kept shooing the same lizard out of my storeroom, he always returning the minute I looked away. So I gave up. I don't really care if he wants to live in there.

But rather than go exploring like Dillard and Thoreau and Leopold, perhaps this pilgrim at Begoso Creek should just sit and wait to see what the land will bring timidly into view. And listen. I hear scamperings and rustlings all around me, but whoever is responsible for these noises seldom lets himself be seen. Anu did find an elk horn this morning in the meadow, but it was old and weatherworn. He has been working on it all day, tossing it and pouncing on it, then sitting and chewing on it, driven to satisfy his insatiable puppy-need to gnaw.

And there are some human sounds too. Every few days I hear one of the Baca brothers down in the meadow by his windmill beyond my gate, herding his cows by honking at them with his truck horn. Fortunately the windmill is a good distance away, so this harsh honking doesn't shatter me. Now and then during the day a jet appears high above the mesa, growling across the sky on its way to Dallas or Chicago or New York City. On Fridays—always only on Fridays, Andelecio tells me—a rancher up on the mesa top takes out his World War II bomber for an outing to Las Vegas.

"I think he just takes it into town to get a cup of coffee," Andy had laughed.

While I was writing this morning, I heard a tremendous roar overhead. It was the bomber—and today is Friday. If the wind is coming my way, I can hear the 10 A.M. westbound AT&SF blowing its horn ten miles away crow-wise at Ribera, slowing down to warn the villagers as it rumbles across the highway and on over the Pecos bridge. It is the coal train from Raton, bringing coal down from York Canyon to Albuquerque and then on to utility stations farther west. These sounds—with perhaps the exception of the Friday bomber—don't bother me. They are rather pleasant. Their effect is to remind me just how far away from them I really am out here in Begoso Canyon.

5

Late this morning I have visitors. In the distance two pickups amble in tandem along the meadow road. They must be neighbors, since only the adjacent ranchers have the keys to the cattle gates. I recognize Andelecio's Chevy, and soon behind it a white Toyota pulls up with two men. One of the men is Seferino, a neighbor who owns the cow pasture just south of me. He lives at the Pueblo gate, across from the old Ortiz place, and keeps an eye on everyone who starts up the road. Andy and Seferino have come to introduce me to Seferino's brother, Elipio, also a neighbor, whose cattle gate I must pass through on my way to the cabin. I offer my guests a beer, and we stand around the dying morning fire, talking of Natividad and his life. They inspect my improvements to the cabin and seem pleased that I have rescued it from its slow deterioration.

"Natividad sure knew how to build a place," says Seferino. "Look at these supports." He slaps his hand approvingly against one of the juniper trunks supporting the *portal* at the notch of a branch. "He put these in dry. If you put juniper in green it will rot. I learned my lesson with juniper on those fence posts I put in on my upper pasture. They only lasted twenty-five years."

After Seferino and Elipio leave, Andy goes over to his truck and brings out a bottle of his homemade wine—*pisado,* he tells me, named for its method of production: stomping barefoot on the grapes to press out the juice. A housewarming present. I stir up the coals in the firepit and set on a couple of logs that soon catch and flare. Although the day is sunny, the April air is fresh enough to make the fire a comfort. We sit together by the fire and share some lunch and the *pisado.* He tells me that his twenty-five-hundred-acre ranch on Rowe Mesa hasn't yet sold, and he wonders if he really wants it to sell. His house in Ribera, where his mother died a few months ago, is also for sale. Although he has spent the last twenty years working in Albuquerque, his roots are in the village and its people.

In the 1700s Andelecio's family migrated from Spain and settled in the river valley near San Miguel. Andy recounts to me stories his grandfather Padilla told him about Comanche raids on the river villages. The Comanche trick for getting meat from the

Spaniards was to climb up on the roof of a house, lower a stick down the chimney, and hook the meat cooking on the hearth. The Comanches took great delight in grabbing the village babies by the feet and smashing their brains against a rock. He tells me his grandfather as an infant was blond, and a Comanche grabbed him out of his cradle one day with great anticipation, thinking he was getting the chance to smash an "Americano." Somehow the screaming women of the household managed to convince him the baby was really a Spaniard, and the Indian dropped him in disappointed disgust.

As a teenager, Andy worked with his uncle on the railroad. One July morning, he tells me, when they were sleeping in a bunk car on a siding in a remote area of central New Mexico, his uncle woke him in the early predawn. Andy saw the world noon-bright with an eerie, uncanny light, the mountains clear as the ones we are looking at in the distance beyond the meadow. It was "The Gadget"—the first atomic test blast.

Later Andy worked at Los Alamos, loading bombs onto trucks and delivering them to defense installations all over the country. One day he was given a special assignment: It had been discovered that for several months a young man from Las Cruces had been making trips to the Trinity test site north of Alamagordo, loading up the pretty green glass-fused rocks into the back of his car, and selling them as souvenir trinkets in Albuquerque. It was Andy's job to stop this trafficking.

"I doubt that poor fool is alive today," Andy says, "and where now are all those rocks he sold?" By now the radioactivity has greatly subsided, but the thought that once the lethal trinitite was sitting out on a trinket shelf somewhere—anywhere—in the country brings a pall of horror over our conversation.

"Do you know the story of Dr. Slotin?" Andy asks me after a

while. The story of Dr. Slotin's heroic action in Los Alamos has become almost legendary in New Mexico, but I didn't know exactly what had happened.

"Were you up there then?" I asked.

"Yes," Andy replied. "Some radioactive material that was being handled by remote controls slipped out of its place while they were making a bomb up in the lab. Slotin rushed in and grabbed it with his bare hands to prevent a disaster. His body was blistered all over. I went to see him in the hospital. A true scientist to the end, he was recording for his colleagues the sensations of the radioactivity in his body. He died three weeks later." Andy stares into the fire for a while and then says, "Sometimes I wonder if the cancer that got me three years ago is related to all that."

Andy's story reminds me of a conversation I had with an elderly waitress a couple of years ago. I had stopped at the Owl Cafe in San Antonio, a tiny village just off I-25, the major north-south artery of the state. The cafe is a local watering hole, as well as a welcome travel stop for drivers weary of the long hot pull from El Paso to Albuquerque across the Jornada del Muerto, the flat, glaring plain of central New Mexico. In the mid-1940s, the waitress told me, the Owl was also the hangout for the government workers at the Trinity test site only thirty miles away.

"One day we realized that the government guys had suddenly cleared out of town," she said. I could hear the note of anger in her voice. "We didn't know why—why they had come or why they left. Everything was very hush-hush. Then that bomb goes off and the sky over San Antonio is brighter than the sun at noon." This is just as Andy had seen it from the bunk car on the railroad siding, some fifteen miles south of San Antonio. Apparently, the Owl's erstwhile customers were safely far away.

My waitress returned to my table to clear the dishes. I could tell she wasn't through airing her anger.

"And if it weren't enough that they drop an atomic bomb thirty miles from here," she continued heatedly, "now they want to dump all their nuclear trash on us! You know—that WIPP site down in Carlsbad." She was referring to the Waste Isolation Pilot Plant, a series of salt caverns dug almost a half mile deep under a ten-thousand-acre site near the Texas–New Mexico border. WIPP is to be a dump for medium-level transuranic waste (a half-life of only twenty-four thousand years) shipped by truck in containers from nuclear weapons facilities across the nation.

"Why can't they take care of their mess where they made it?" my waitress went on angrily. "Why haul it across all those highways and through all those cities to dump it here?"

Indeed many New Mexicans are asking the same thing and more. Is the WIPP site safe enough to hold the planned million barrels of waste without leaking over the next thousands of years? There are reports of brine leaking into the tunnels, concern about whether the shipping barrels will hold up en route in a traffic accident, questions of possible gas generation and explosion from the decaying waste, of the future safety of the aquifer that overlies the caverns and feeds into the Pecos River. WIPP was scheduled to open several years ago, but so far these questions have held up the start of shipments. At least we can ask—but Congress has ensured through its WIPP legislation that the state will have no veto power over the project.

I recount my Owl Cafe story to Andy.

"Yes," he says, resignedly. "I guess a lot of folks in Washington see the land of New Mexico as simply expendable." We have both been reading the newspaper stories that are appearing lately: of contaminated canyons draining the Pajarito Plateau around Los Alamos; of lost dump sites around the laboratory—lost because accurate records weren't kept during the forties and fifties of where the nuclear waste was buried; of deliberate release of radioactive emissions to test how far they would travel; of possibly a higher-than-normal incidence of brain tumors and other cancers around Los Alamos and downstream in Rio Arriba County; allegations that the lab used its own employees as unwitting guinea pigs to test their tolerance to radiation exposure. I think of Andy's cancer. I hope he wasn't one of these.

"Of course," Andy continues, "the lab says all these things are mistakes of the past. Nothing like this is going on now."

"Let's hope so!" I counter. "But that mess up there may be around forever."

Later, after Andy has left, these thoughts intrude as I take my evening walk with Anu down to the ranch gate before dinner. How do I reconcile the world as I "know" it to be with the beauty before my eyes? I want to live like that legendary Navajo: beauty above him, beauty below him, beauty before him. Our generation knows so much. Perhaps, in some ways, we know too much. We know what the Navajo only felt. Our knowledge makes us see the world differently from the Navajo, or from Natividad. We know all about our beautiful fragile environment—why the world of Begoso Canyon is the way it is. Why Anu's beetles and magpies. Why the coyotes sing in the morning. Why the junipers are sneaking back into the meadow. Why the plants in the meadow are the ones that must be here, must live in this particular embracing association in this particular meadow, on this particular soil, in this climate, at this elevation, at this latitude, at this particular time in the cycles of their succession. Our science has brought us our understanding of these things. And we also know why it is imperative that we must save these things, if they—and we—are to continue to be. But what we don't know is how to deal with the mess we've made.

I'm sure this issue never came up for Natividad. I doubt he ever heard the word "environment"—*el medio ambiente*. Natividad probably spoke no English, or if he did it would have been minimal. But the word would not have been there for him in either language. His was a world of trees and rocks, sun, snow, rain, and critters— elements to be conquered. Only to our generation do these things add up to an "environment." Natividad was a pioneer, and as for all pioneers these things were, in the words of Aldo Leopold, "the raw materials out of which he hammered the artifact of civilization."[1] And he was successful. And just because he was successful, his suc- ceeding generation has come to know what it knows. Certainly Na- tividad and his kind created problems for the land through their ignorance: overgrazed pastures, depleted forests and soils, eroded waterways. Indeed, I can see signs of this abuse even here in Begoso Canyon. But these are things that, through our knowledge, can be recovered. We can afford to admire the achievements of our fore- bears, admire them because these achievements—we now know— were limited, not irreversibly destructive. But we have now carried these hard-wrought achievements beyond bounds. Natividad could only control to a point the raw elements from which he hammered the artifact of his civilization. He didn't know enough to really mess things up. His trash heap, which I find so entertaining, in our gen- eration has become the nuclear waste dump. We've pushed things over the edge, out of control.

But still, I muse as I approach the ranch gate, Natividad, as an individual, must have been special. His grandparents were Indians, and perhaps he had something of that Navajo who walked in beauty

about him. He could have stayed in the village with his brothers and sisters, and just come out here on his horse to tend his sheep and beans. But he didn't. With great effort he built himself a stone cabin, piled up more of those heavy stones to build a sheep corral, dug with his own hands a well, planted his corn and beans, and lived here alone in Begoso Canyon. He may have been an ornery old cuss—opinion in the village is divided on this—but I can't believe that he worked so hard, already in the first half of the twentieth century, if he didn't have a need to live here in beauty. Still today no one has built a house anywhere near here. The closest house is now, as it was then, down in the village.

I close my mind on these thoughts because I have no answer to them. Despite the curse we have laid on this land, the beauty is not yet destroyed. And I am here in Begoso Canyon, in Natividad's canyon. And while God is still putting up with us, still handing out blessings, I will grab mine and walk here in beauty as Natividad did, as that long-ago Navajo did.

ᘓ

The distant ridge directly east above the Pecos Valley is watermelon pink in the late afternoon light, pocked with dark polka dots of pine. To the south, Rowe Mesa is glowing at its crest, a dark shadow working up its shoulder from below. As I reach the gate, Baca's cows moo at me—perhaps in greeting or perhaps annoyance, or maybe they don't even know why they moo what they moo. At the gate I call Anu to turn back. We will walk back on the road this time, the hour too late to take the longer way along the creek bottom back to the cabin. The setting sun is sitting on the Punta de la Flecha, the arrow-shaped point above the village of San Jose where the mesa wall makes its turn from west to south. In this brilliant, last-gasp glare I am blinded to the fore-ridges that I know are there, that divide the space in front of me from the top. On the road, a dry curly juniper twig flashes into a snake and then back into a twig again in front of my sun-glazed eyes. The air around me is so bright I can't see the cabin, usually in plain sight from here. At the point where Seferino's road cuts south from mine to take him to his upper pasture, I look forward into the glare and see my Toyota explode into brilliance. It is the only thing I can see as I face the sun. As I approach closer, the truck windows implode back to their places, their sudden moment of brilliance extinguished as the sun finally drops below the edge of the mesa. The truck, the cabin, the trees and ridges—the environment—become visible again.

The fire is still smoldering in the pit when I return. I am hungry. I don't bother with the stove tonight and just warm my dinner on the grill—leftover rice and tuna from my lunch with Andy. Topped with half a can of tomatoes and a shake of Parmesan, dinner is a treat.

Natividad's homestead occupies a tiny portion of what were once the common lands of the San Miguel del Bado community land grant. It was a royal grant—*una merced real*—and the land that it once encompassed is still called the *merced* by the villagers. Living on the old grant, I was curious to find out its history. I spent several hours reading in the Santa Fe library.

In 1794 the king's governor in Santa Fe received a petition from

Lorenzo Marquez and fifty-one other settlers—some of whom were *genizaros,* that is, Christianized Indians—for a large tract of land that stretched from a few miles east of the pueblo at Pecos over to what is now the village of Bernal, taking in many miles along the northern reaches of the Pecos River. It was an area that, when later surveyed, was found to comprise 315,000 acres. The governor approved the settlers' request and instructed the alcalde of Santa Fe— an official similar to a judicial magistrate or mayor—to allot small, approximately ten-acre parcels along the river to each of the families. These small parcels were to be privately owned and could be bought and sold. The remaining land was set aside for future settlers and as common land to be used by all the settlers for grazing and as a source of firewood and building material. Among the conditions of the grant, Marquez and his companions were to build a fortified plaza, set aside land to build a church, and construct the acequias, or ditches, to irrigate their crops.

The population of the new *merced* grew quickly. New villages sprang up along the river. After a few years there were so many people using the land that San Miguel settlers petitioned the government for new grants. First, Anton Chico and Tecolote, and then in 1835 Las Vegas, east of San Miguel at the edge of the Great Plains.

San Miguel's heyday came when Mexico claimed independence from Spain in 1821. The new government opened the Santa Fe Trail, and San Miguel became the port of entry into Mexican territory for the U.S. traders coming from Missouri to Santa Fe. The traces of the trail, where it forded the Pecos and entered the plaza, are still visible today, as Andy had pointed out when we first came out to see the Begoso cabin. The village supplied the travelers with lodging and food, saloons and a brothel, as well as a blacksmith and supplies to restock the wagons. The government charged a duty of five hundred dollars per wagon when the traders arrived in Santa Fe; hence the traders often spent several days in San Miguel, repacking the wagons to cut down the number before entering the capital. Troops were stationed at the San Miguel garrison, both to protect the villages and to escort the wagons to Santa Fe to ensure that the trail taxes were paid.

After the Americans took over the territory in 1846, San Miguel's fortunes fell. Just east of Las Vegas, the Americans built Fort Union, the major distribution facility for all the newly acquired Southwest territories. The fort not only supplied jobs and a market for local goods but also provided the eastern plains with protection from Indian attacks, allowing the town of Las Vegas and the surrounding lands to develop. When the Atcheson, Topeka, and Santa Fe Railroad came through the area in 1879, Las Vegas quickly became a major shipping center. The railroad didn't bother with a station at San Miguel, only a water tank—which is still there today—along the tracks at Ribera, half a mile north of the plaza.

But even the train was not the final blow that turned San Miguel into the collection of crumbling ruins that still dot the edges of the old plaza. At the end of the century, the people lost the common lands of the *merced* by decision of the U.S. Supreme Court. All that was left of the 315,000 acres after the Court's decision were about 5,000 acres that could be claimed by the people who had been living there or who were heirs of people living there at the time of the Treaty of Guadalupe in 1848.

New Mexicans are very aware that during the second half of the nineteenth century, many of the land grants, both those made to individuals and those to communities, were swindled away from their rightful owners. Congress, whose role it was to confirm ownership of these grants, was far away from the territory. It could only rely on the information submitted by the U.S. agents charged to investigate the claims. Unfortunately many of these agents, and the lawyers they worked with, were corrupt, working to dispossess the owners and grab the land for themselves and their friends. The San Miguel grant, however, was not lost through the chicanery of corrupt lawyers. Rather, it was the Supreme Court's decision that the common lands be taken over by the U.S. government as public domain.

One day when I stopped at Ribera to pick up my mail, I ran into Andelecio in the post office. I told him I had just been reading about the *merced* and asked him if he could fill in some of the gaps in the story.

"Well I'll tell you what I know anyway," he said. "Come on over to the house and we'll get some coffee."

I sat down at the kitchen table, and Andy poured us each a cup of coffee from the pot on the woodstove. "Did you know it was my great-uncle, Julian Sandoval, who fought all the way to the Supreme Court to keep the San Miguel grant for the people? My folks were always proud of that, even though he couldn't win the case."

"What happened that the people lost?" I asked. "I read that the papers confirming the grant back in 1794 were all recorded with the Spanish governor."

"Oh, there was no question that the papers were all in order. Both the first surveyor general and later the Court of Private Land Claims decided in favor of the community."

"So who appealed to the Supreme Court?"

"The way I heard it," said Andy, "when the Private Land Claims Court supported the community's claim, everyone thought that was that. Then the U.S. attorney appealed to the Supreme Court. He argued that the common land ought to belong to the U.S. government as public domain."

"But what about the Treaty of Guadalupe? Didn't the U.S. promise to protect the ownership of the land grants?"

"That's what people are still mad about. Not just here but all over New Mexico. In our case, the Supreme Court decided the common land really didn't belong to the people in the first place. The justices argued that originally the common land was still held legally by the king of Spain, and so then later by the Mexican government, and so now by the U.S. government. The people got 5,000 acres out of the deal, which was just a little more than what they were all living on anyway. So the grant still officially exists, but that's all there is of it."

"So how did Natividad get the homestead out in Begoso Canyon? Didn't that part go to the U.S. as public domain?"

"It's really ironic," Andy said. "The government took over the land, then turned around and offered most of it back again as 160-acre homesteads. They kept the steep areas of Rowe Mesa and gave that to the Forest Service. But a lot of people were able to claim some land back again."

"But what could you do with 160 acres of homestead in an arid place like this? That might be enough land to run a farm in Iowa or Ohio, but here you'd need hundreds, maybe thousands of acres to be able to keep enough sheep or cows to make a living."

"Exactly," said Andy. "If you didn't have the money to buy more land you lost out completely. People just left and never came back." Andy brought the coffeepot over from the stove and poured us another cup.

"People grabbed the good pasture and water holes first,"

he continued. "So what had been open to everyone was suddenly chopped up and closed off with barbed wire fences. People had to dig wells and negotiate easements. It was the Anglo way of doing things, and it just didn't work here."

"What about Natividad?" I asked.

"Well, Natividad could make it on his homestead parcel because he had no family to support, and anyway, all he wanted was to be a hermit. He lived a kind of hand-to-mouth existence out there all alone. He had his corn and beans and his vegetable garden down by the well, and some sheep and goats he could sell if he needed money. And he could shoot deer or rabbits or even a snake for dinner. And don't forget he was gone for a long time. Even he couldn't hold out during the depression."

Andy was quiet for a while, drinking his coffee. Then he said, "Natividad was such a loner, a real hermit. I remember when he came back from Nevada in the fifties. He was already old, but he just wanted to be out there in the canyon by himself. My folks kind of kept an eye on him. Whenever my mother baked bread, she would bake some extra for Natividad. My father would take it out to him and take him some of our homemade wine."

"Was he friendly?" I asked. I had heard stories about how cantankerous he could be.

"Well, he didn't get along with everyone around here, and he sure didn't want people coming out to the canyon and bothering him. But he got along with my family just fine. I used to go out there and talk to him sometimes. His life was about as simple as you can get, but some people around here thought he was pretty weird."

Andy's remark made me think of a visit I had one afternoon shortly after I had moved into the cabin. One of my neighbors brought his ancient mother out to the canyon for a Sunday drive in his pickup. They stopped to say hello. I had just finished washing clothes in the big galvanized tin tub that doubles as my bathtub and was hanging the clothes to dry on the hog fence. The old woman looked at the cabin and then at me with my laundry, and asked, "Vivas acqui sola?" It was a simple enough question, but I wasn't sure if the look on her face was one of disbelief or just plain disapproval. Perhaps both. But her attitude made me feel I had a special bond with Natividad.

Often friends ask me if I don't get lonely living in such a remote place. No, I am not lonely in Begoso Canyon. But how can I explain to people who don't see things in the same way I do? For me there is a sense of gentle embrace. The landscape is quiet and somehow humane; the stars, in their incredible high-desert clarity, are vast, and yet they seem to be there for me. I am engaged in this world: with the sunrise and the sunset. With the quiet snow, with the pounding hail, with the hot dry wind. There is so much to observe and to wonder at that there is little space left for loneliness.

But perhaps the most important reason I am not lonely is Anu. I am constantly aware of his presence. His level of consciousness is sufficient to contact me, yet I am forever grateful that he can't talk. I do know that if he were not with me, I would indeed be lonely, but I have never come to Begoso without him. One friend asked me if I sometimes start talking to myself. Certainly not, I answered. I talk to Anu.

I told Andy about my ancient visitor. "Sure," he laughed. "That must have been old Antonia Baca. You are probably incomprehensible to her. She must be wondering why anyone would choose to live like you do out there when you don't have to."

Of course to choose to live the primitive life is one thing; to be forced to live it is another. From her age, I would guess that Antonia probably grew up under conditions similar to what she saw at my cabin. I can well imagine that it made no sense to her for someone to step backward from the relatively comfortable improvements of modernity into that early way of life. Several months before, while I was waiting for the problems relating to my purchase of the land to be cleared up, I borrowed the gate keys from Andy and brought a friend out to see my find. She had grown up in just such a place in another part of northern New Mexico. My enthusiasm was lost on her.

"All the time I was growing up," Lisa said with a grimace, "I wanted to get away from a place like this." She now lives in Santa Fe in a very fine house indeed.

"Thanks for the coffee," I said to Andy, gathering up my mail from the kitchen table. "And for the history lesson, too."

Andy walked me out to my truck. "You can look up that court case about my great-uncle in the library," he said. "Maybe reading the case will help you sort out some of the details of the story."

🙰

When I returned to Santa Fe a few days later, I went to the State Archives to see what more I could find out about the loss of the San Miguel grant. I started with the 1897 case of *United States v. Sandoval et al.*[2] It was just as Andy had told me. The Court decided the land never had belonged legally to the people. The case not only spelled the end of common ownership of the San Miguel del Bado grant, it was a turning point in land grant litigation in New Mexico. Before the *Sandoval* case, Congress had confirmed a few of the community grants to the people who lived on them. But after *Sandoval*, all other common lands were taken over by the federal government as public domain.

In the archives I also found some unsavory twists to the San

Miguel story that went far beyond the Supreme Court decision. The San Miguel del Bado grant almost fell victim to the notorious Santa Fe Ring, a group of land-grabbing lawyers and corrupt government agents, sometimes with the self-serving complicity of Hispanic *ricos,* who used whatever means necessary to get possession of the land grants for themselves. Often the game was to trick illiterate owners into signing away their property, not realizing what they were doing. Another was to impose taxes on the property and, when the owners couldn't pay, to force them out. And if an owner or a community of owners hired a lawyer to help them, the lawyer usually helped himself to a third of the grant as his fee.

The U.S. surveyor general, Henry Atkinson, was a member of the Ring. In 1879 Atkinson made the specious argument to Congress that since the original list of names of the petitioners in 1794, with the exception of Lorenzo Marquez, was lost, the entire San Miguel grant should belong only to the heirs of Marquez. This, despite the fact that the final list of names confirming ownership in 1803 was intact. Congress took no action on Atkinson's report, perhaps finally beginning to smell the proverbial rat. Nevertheless, suddenly all the Marquez family holdings were bought up. The deeds passed through several hands, finally landing in the pockets of Levi Morton, formerly a member of Congress and later vice-president of the United States under Benjamin Harrison. Morton had undoubtedly heard Atkinson's report when he was in Congress. He tried to use the report to argue that since he was now the owner of all the private parcels that had belonged to the Marquez heirs, the entire 315,000-acre grant should go to him. The Supreme Court heard Morton's argument along with that of Uncle Julian for the community and the U.S. attorney's argument that the land should become public domain. The Court saw through the fishiness of Morton's claim and denied him.[3] But all the villagers got out of the case were 5,024 acres. And later the chance to claim small pieces of the common land back as homesteads.

The next Sunday, on my way to the cabin, I stopped by Andelecio's house to tell him what I had found out.

claim and denied him.[3] But all the villagers got out of the case were 5,024 acres. And later the chance to claim small pieces of the common land back as homesteads.

The next Sunday, on my way to the cabin, I stopped by Andelecio's house to tell him what I had found out.

"It's pretty disgusting," I said, as we sat having coffee again in his kitchen, "that not only were so many of the government agents corrupt, but even the man who soon would be the next vice-president was trying to swindle these people out of their land."

Andy just laughed. "Seems like that sort of thing still goes on all the time, wouldn't you say?"

"Okay, okay. You're right there," I conceded. "But why do you think the U.S. government took away the *merced* and then turned around and offered most of it back again to largely the same people who had claimed it before, but now in more or less useless small chunks?"

Andy was quiet for a moment, his chin cupped in his hand. Finally he looked up. "Perhaps the only answer is the Anglo mind-set of legal order," he suggested. "Common ownership was a well-established tenet of Spanish and Mexican law. But Washington probably saw it as too imprecise, too legally messy. Maybe the Americans just couldn't deal with the idea that a loose collection of people could jointly own the land. The Anglo mind needed land to be divided up into precise townships and ranges and sections and quarters, neatly fenced off by barbed wire, and deeded in identifiable parcels, recorded on a piece of paper. Private property was sacred; common property was confusion."

I had to agree with him. Private property is the sacred cow of our culture. Good fences make good neighbors. Alas, there have even been times in our recent history when the idea of communal land would have been viewed with suspicion by some in our government as a subversive plot. We pride ourselves on our individualism. We can even be generous, like the great philanthropists, and give things away. But we seem to have a lot of trouble simply sharing.

Driving out along the canyon road after leaving Andy's, I thought about Lorenzo Marquez and his fellow settlers claiming all this land two hundred years ago. They had made their claim in the traditional manner: walking over the grant with the alcalde, picking up rocks and bunches of grass and tossing them about, shouting "Viva el Rey de España!" Possession was achieved as simply as that. And I thought how that simple ritual, which guaranteed the Hispanic people their means of livelihood, would, a century later, precipitate such greed and unconscionable corruption in the people of another culture.

7

The steep wall of Rowe Mesa curves from west to south at the Punta de la Flecha, high above my cabin. There is something thrilling about living in the presence of a magnificent geologic formation. You feel chosen to be present at a sacred mystery, at a subtle moment of eternity, when the universe softens its indifference and draws you into its magic. Perhaps the Indians who fished the waters below Yosemite Falls felt this way, or those who watched the fingers of the morning sun descend, inch by inch, into the depths of the Grand Canyon, erasing the shadows of night and bathing the orange sandstone cliffs in brilliance. Probably the consensus would not equate Rowe Mesa with Yosemite Valley or the Grand Canyon.

Still, for me, the mesa partakes of that sacral quality that Nature, in her most imposing revelations, deigns to confer. We are permitted to bear witness. We are chosen.

At Glorieta Pass, thirty miles to the west of my cabin, Rowe Mesa rises abruptly along the south side of the Santa Fe–Las Vegas freeway. In 1541 Francisco Vásquez de Coronado's expedition skirted the mesa and crossed through Glorieta Pass in the fruitless attempt to discover the legendary seven golden cities of Cibola. Centuries later, the pass was the scene of slaughter, the most westerly battle-field of the Civil War. Here, in March 1862, the Colorado Volunteers, led by Maj. John Chivington, attacked the Confederate supply train and forced General Sibley and his straggle of troops to retreat to Texas, thus smashing the Confederate dream of an empire of gold and silver stretching to the Pacific. The bones of the hapless Confederates were discovered by chance just a few years ago in a mass grave, unearthed by someone working a bull-dozer. Many of the battlefield trees are imbedded with musket shells, now much scabbed over after a century and more, except for those trees whose trunks have been gouged by the knives of souvenir hunters.

East beyond the pass, the mesa falls in a steep escarpment, un-dulating between five hundred and a thousand feet above the high-way. The walls are striated with horizontal lines of paleozoic brick-red sandstone and hard, yellowish limestone layered with softer mudstone and siltstone—a testimony to the ebb and flow of the an-cient seas that covered this part of New Mexico millions of years ago. Even though the walls are covered now with trees, the layers are still clearly visible. At the Punta, below which the Pecos River crosses under the highway, flowing full from its source in the San-gre de Cristo Mountains, the mesa abruptly turns and follows the river south, forming the west wall of the Upper Pecos Valley.

The relationship between the mesa and the river comes to a falling out a few miles downstream from the village of El Pueblo, ending their joint enterprise—the mesa rising up, the river cutting through. Beyond this point the river flows on to irrigate the fields along its banks, downstream past Anton Chico, Puerto de Luna, and south across the central plains of New Mexico. Nine hundred miles from its source on the slopes of Pecos Baldy, the Pecos flows into the Rio Grande on the Tex-Mex border. In its northern reaches, the Pecos is the line between the plains and the mountains. It was also the Maginot Line of Comanche territory, and the Spanish people of the valley often acknowledge—now with pride, but perhaps not at the time—a Comanche grandfather or great-uncle in the family.

The escarpment of the mesa gradually disappears into the leveling contours. From my cabin, I can see only the curve of the mesa wall that faces northeast. The top is a vast flatness, covered with ponderosa and fir, sparsely dotted with ranches and an occasional, now almost destitute, village. On the U.S. Geological Survey maps for this part of the world, the escarpment is depicted from quad to quad in a series of tight wiggles and humps, the humps announcing the descent of a waterway. My cabin crouches at the foot of this wiggling monster, tucked into a crease between its toes. I live in the magic of its shadow.

᠎᠎᠎

Wednesday evening I sat by the fire and watched the orange moon pull up the night from behind the dim shadow of Bernal Ridge above the Pecos. It is already early May. There was a late frost the night before, but Wednesday evening was clear and fresh. Later in the night, whenever I awoke to adjust my tormented back on Natividad's miserable cot, I could see a bright, star-filled sky through the little window above my bed.

And then the dawn broke blue and clear. I rejoice in anticipation of another lovely day. Today I will plant the vines I brought out from a friend's nursery—silver lace and wisteria and grape, hardy vines that I hope will withstand my neglect. I will plant them along Anu's hog fence.

I should know better. By ten o'clock the New Mexico weather has pulled one of its tricks: it is snowing, a cold wind rattling the stovepipes above the roof. So the vines will have to wait. This will be a day for inside chores—dusting the shelves and sweeping the stone floors clean of the sand that continuously drifts down from the river-plastered walls. And perhaps finishing the lace curtains for the windows. I started them more than a month ago. Lace curtains may sound elegantly out of place for this humble cabin, but their purpose is quite functional. They screen out mosquitos and flies in the summer when the windows are open and obscure the contents of the cabin from the nosiness of some passing hunter when I'm not here. And then when I finish them, I can sit out the snowstorm in grandmother's ugly rocking chair and read by the stove.

By noon, however, the snow has stopped and the sun is licking up the last of the gray clouds. I haven't finished the curtains, but I'd better get those vines in while the ground is still wet. I spend the afternoon digging, planting the vines and tying their trailers onto the hog wire. And just in time. The sun has disappeared again, and I feel the first drops of rain. And then the deluge comes. I duck back into the cabin, glad that the vines will get a good soaking start in their new life.

But I have a problem. I told Andelecio that I would drive out to Ribera this evening to talk over some things and look at some old

maps he has. But now with the pouring rain, I know the dirt road will soon turn to muddy slush. Driving in the caliche mud of New Mexican dirt roads can be difficult and dangerous. A light truck like mine can easily fishtail in the muck. At first I decide against leaving, assuming that Andy will understand why I don't show up. But I do want to see those maps. What to do?

And then I hit on Natividad's sheep corral. Of course—the answer to the muck: those huge stones. I put the pickup into four-wheel low and drive it across the soggy meadow to the corral. I load up the back with as many big stones as I can fit on the truckbed—ten or twelve big stones should add maybe five hundred pounds of ballast to keep the truck from sliding. When I have lifted all the rocks, I pick up my wet and squirming puppy and put him in the cab seat next to me. We take off slowly down the dirt road, stopping in the rain to open then close all the five gates on the way to the paved highway. The dirt of the road is not yet saturated. These storms don't usually last long, so if the rain lets up, I'll be fine. The truck rides smoothly, the ballast keeping it on course. I am feeling rather proud of myself for having so easily solved the mud problem.

It's still raining heavily when I get to Andy's. Andy and I sit in his kitchen and look at his old ownership maps of properties in Begoso Canyon. He shows me where there were once, years ago, some old homesteads farther up the canyon beyond my place. These must be the ruins I've encountered on my hiking explorations. Anu is under the kitchen table glued to my leg, nervously avoiding the monster lurking in the woodbox behind the woodstove. While we are talking, I glance out the window to see if the rain has stopped. Indeed it has: it has turned to snow. Heavy slushy snow that will sit for a few minutes on my dirt road and then slowly soak deep into it, making the oozing, treacherous caliche far worse than when I drove out.

I tell Andy that I had better leave immediately. I pry Anu loose from my leg and take him out to the truck. It is already dark. I drive the five miles of paved highway back to the Pueblo gate, the relentless snow making vision almost impossible in the glare of the headlights. I close and lock the big gate behind me and gun the truck forward as fast as I can, feeling the wheels lurching wherever they please in the butterlike mud. If the ballast in the back is having any beneficial effect, I am not aware of it. In stretches where the road surface is rocky, I'm fine. But in the flat smooth meadows, the truck slides every which way, ignoring my contortions at the steering wheel. I am snow-soaked from stopping to get out and open and close the cattle gates.

I know this road well by now, and I fear that the real test may come some three miles along, not too far this side of the cabin, where the road makes a sharp turn just as it crosses a pipe culvert over an arroyo in Baca's cow pasture. When I get to this last turn, I stop and get out in the snow and walk in the shafts of light from the truck beams to the arroyo to plan my attack. There are two theories of driving in mud: one is you crawl ever so slowly; the other is you gun forward at full speed. I consider the situation and decide on the crawl. I return to the truck, shift to four-wheel low, and inch ahead toward the culvert. I can feel the wheels refusing direction, sliding out of control toward the six-foot drop-off to the arroyo below. I switch fast to theory number two and push the gas pedal to the floor. The truck jerks forward, churning mud up onto the windows, taking the turn crosswise. One rear wheel claws at the creek edge, then finally grabs on and the truck is propelled, flying, into the muddy meadow. But I am safe. I look down at Anu. He has buried his head in his paws and his little brown body is jerking with fear. I run my hand along his quaking back and talk to him softly, as much to calm myself as to calm him, promising him I will never try something this stupid again.

When both Anu and I have sufficiently calmed down, I get out and rub a spy hole with my gloves on the mud-splattered windshield. Then I start the engine and bounce the truck back up onto the road, extremely grateful that the axles are still in one piece. I am chagrined that in my naïveté I presumed to conquer New Mexico mud merely by packing my pickup with stones. Begoso Canyon has much to teach me.

℃

Today is Sunday and I must leave for a while to return to my other life in Santa Fe. I eat my last apple and warm up last night's leftover soup for breakfast: canned kale and tomatoes in ramen, the ramen slushy after sitting in the pot all night. (I must remember to get that granola.) I dump out Anu's water bowl and my environmentally correct dishwater on the chokecherry hedge. Then I go out to the truck and drag out the heavy ballast stones from my adventure of a few nights ago. The sun has been shining steadily for almost three days now, so the road will be dry again. Unlike Natividad, I tie up my plastic garbage bag and pick up the box of empty cans and my visitors' beer bottles and put them in my mud-covered truck to take to town. I think I will stop in the village on the way out and negotiate with Seferino for a cord of firewood. And then drop by Andy's again to discuss a new hand pump for the well—he found one cheap in a mail-order catalog. And since it's Sunday and the old church in San Miguel is open for business, maybe I'll stop and put in a word for Natividad's eternal rest—so well-deserved after his years of work conquering Begoso Canyon. And then I will pull onto the Santa Fe highway and drive west beneath the ancient pine-dotted shores of Rowe Mesa.

PART

Living
the
Seasons

TWO

1

I can't remember when I took it into my head that I would like to live like a hermit. Or at least a sort of semihermit—I have been always too engaged in life to be a candidate for true hermithood. But the desire to withdraw to the wilds has been part of my life for as long as I can remember. Of course we are all many different people at once, and over a lifetime it was easy enough to shove my hermit inclinations to the back burner and engage life as a student, a worker, a friend, wife, mother. During one of the back-burner periods, I even went through a stint as a political activist. I sneaked into a House Un-American Activities Committee hearing one afternoon in 1959 while my fellow students were being fire-hosed down the marble staircase of city hall by San Francisco's finest. The disgusting charade inside the hearing room, along with the screams outside the barred door, awakened in me an intensity of patriotism I hadn't known I was capable of. I became a picketer for worthy causes from ban-the-bomb to down-with-war-toys, a sitter-in at Woolworth's, a writer of outraged letters to besieged editors. And since the leader of the HUAC protest was my love of the moment, he gave his arresting officer my address and phone number as to where he could be found. I am no doubt still listed in some FBI file as a collaborator of movements un-American.

But always there was the hermit side working in me. The desire to somehow, somewhere live the utterly simple life. And the nagging feeling that the things I was doing in those early years, although I believed in them and still do, were ultimately distractions. Even later, the most intimate of human contacts—loverhood, wifehood, motherhood—though love-filled and passionately so, were still distractions from a different reality.

I got my first chance to play my hermit role when I married a young Finnish graduate student and we set out for the Arctic: he to do an ethnographic study of the Lapps that would earn him his doctorate; me to help as I might, but mainly to search for that simple life in a log cabin six hundred kilometers above the Arctic Circle.

And I did indeed find it. It was reindeer country. In late fall we bought our winter food on the hoof. It was my husband Bert's job to stab the poor beast in the heart, drain his blood into a bucket, disembowel him, and trample his intestines in the snow. It was my job to turn him into food. With the advice of the Lapp women, with whom I spoke a broken Finnish, I learned how to make blood bread, how to bake the tongue, how to fill the trampled intestines with liver mixed with rice and raisins. The rice and raisins (as well as flour, sugar, tea, and coffee) were fetched from the Norwegian trading post at Kirkenes on the Berents Sea, two days north by reindeer sled. The parts of the deer that we didn't process, we simply froze in the woodshed in usable-size chunks.

Then in the spring, we did the same to the summer deer. It was very important to kill the animal at precisely the right time so that the meat could be dried on top of the roof. The weather must be too warm for it to freeze and too cold for it to rot. In the summer we fished and salted down for winter what we didn't eat; in the fall we picked buckets of lingon berries, which are loaded with vitamin C and will preserve in their own juice.

Many days and nights in that little log cabin, I had the opportunity to indulge in the delights of hermithood. Traveling in the Arctic could take days, maybe weeks. So I was often alone while Bert went off on skis or reindeer sled to other Lapp settlements to do his research. The only glitch in the joy I felt at this wonderful solitude was that in the Arctic there is no concept of privacy. Shelter and warmth are a matter of life or death and are available to all by right. Many evenings I would be sitting alone by the fire when, without so much as a knock, a stranger would open the cabin door and walk in, grunt a greeting at me, unpack and eat his rye bread and dried reindeer meat, unroll his bedroll by the fire, and sack out. I understood that such hospitality was expected of me, but I was never comfortable with these Arctic intrusions. They assaulted my need for aloneness.

The marriage didn't survive the Arctic. Nor did that Arctic world survive the later twentieth century. Now there are roads and automobiles, electric lights, central heating, Chernobyl fallout, and tourists. But the beauty of living in that frozen world, the learning to survive on the plenty that was out there in the environment never left me.

A few years later I tried my luck with someone from the opposite end of the world. I married a Peruvian. In the twenty years of his growing up until he left Peru for school in the United States, César never found any reason to venture beyond the urban limits of Lima. His idea of the wilderness was as a pretty scene to be observed from the porch of a lodge somewhere, gin-and-tonic in hand. We communicated about other things.

During those years I worked as an urban planner—a curious choice of profession for a closet hermit. But as soon as our two boys were old enough to carry a pack, I took them alone summers to the high country. I felt that of all maternal responsibilities, the most important was to offer my children the wilderness. And they understood: Rafael has become a professional rock climber; Tonio lives in cyberspace, but he knows the mountains are always out there whenever he needs them.

Beyond my own experiences of withdrawal to the wilds, however, perhaps I am also a child of the times—a woman child of woman times. In the past few years there has emerged what one might call a genre of withdrawal-to-nature literature written by women who have severed—either completely or at least substantially—their dependence on urban life. Certainly over the years many women have lived alone in the wilds and some have written about their lives. But recently more and more women want to talk about their experiences, to tell us their stories.

I suppose to some extent the desire of these women to retreat from a hectic urban world, as well as to want to tell us about it, is a result of a feminist movement that has given women the self-confidence to say to this world of presumed equal opportunity: "Hey, I can do that too." But I think there is more to it than feminist pride. These are the stories of women who have chosen to get out of the "system," to find their reality in nature, to experience a very private freedom. Sue Hubbell, who writes of her life as a keeper of bees in the Ozarks, has put her finger on it as well as anyone:

> *It is a good time to be a grown-up woman with individuality, strength and crotchets. We are wonderfully free. Our children are the independent adults we helped them to be-*

*come, and though they may still want our love, they don't
need our care. Social rules are so flexible today that nothing
we do is shocking. There are no political barriers to us anymore. Provided we stay healthy and can support ourselves,
we can do anything, have anything, and spend our talents
as we please.*[1]

Some of these women writers have mates — or off and on have
mates — others are alone. Some earn their living from the wilds,
some have other incomes or live from their writing. But whatever
their work once was, it usually took place in a city. To name just a
few: Dorothy Gilman, who called her New York life "a slow death
of the spirit," fled her publishing job to weather the storms of Nova
Scotia. Gretel Ehrlich, a public television filmmaker, went on location in Wyoming and never went back; Sue Hubbell was a university
librarian before she switched to bees; and Pulitzer Prize–winner
Annie Dillard's solitary musings along the banks of Tinker Creek
have become a classic of contemporary literature. But perhaps the
grandmother of us all is Anne Morrow Lindbergh. My father gave
me her *Gift from the Sea* when I was a teenager. His gift made me
realize how well he knew me.

For some women, the pain of divorce drove them into their
new life. Maybe at first they just ran — as far away as possible. And
when the pain subsided, they found themselves surrounded by a
beauty so powerful and life-changing, they could never go back. I
once stopped in a bar-cafe in a tiny rural New Mexican village. It
was late and I was tired; I had been driving for hours. As I climbed
onto the bar stool of this windswept, woebegone, and quite empty
establishment, I was amazed to find the barkeep an elegant, urbane,

and very beautiful woman. She had run too. From a home in Beverly Hills and a divorce. A skilled horsewoman, she spends her days herding sheep with the Basque ranchers in the area and her nights running the bar. You can find one of us most anywhere.

My retreat to the banks of Begoso Creek is not a story of divorce but of a more permanent separation. César, ever the absent-minded professor, drifted across the centerline of a highway in Spain, and my life as I had known it came to an end. At first I went back to my office: I suppose an office is as good or as bad a place as any to deal with the pain, the emptiness, the bizarre dreams of crashing cars, the nightly visitations of ghosts. But in time these feelings, these nightmares can be corralled and tied down. Life becomes livable again. Time to quit the job, sell the house, cash in the retirement funds, and run.

New Mexico was the logical place for me to run to. César and I had always planned to live here. For me, it was the vastness that drew me, the brilliance of the afternoon light, the suddenness of rain, the gentle ruggedness of the land. For him, the Hispanic culture made him feel comfortable, almost like being at home again, but with the touch of U.S. order and rationality that he admired. Once, when we were nearly out of gas on a mountain road, we found a gas pump out in front of an old adobe farmhouse. César addressed the ancient farmer in Spanish and was addressed in return as "Vuestra Merced"—a deference that in Spain or Latin America hasn't been used on ordinary mortals since the seventeenth century. This confirmed for César that we must move here. "I want to live," he said, "where I can talk to people who talk like that."

He never got the chance. It was for me to pick up that dream and run with it. All the way to Begoso Canyon.

2

One August afternoon, by the sun clock close to six, I started the fire in the firepit. It would take a good half hour for the coals to be right for cooking my dinner, so I called Anu and we walked down to the ranch gate. The sun was still warm and the afternoon wind had died down in the canyon. When we reached the gate and turned to walk back, I felt the wind start to pick up again. I could see the smoke from the firepit rising in the distance. Concerned about the untended fire, I began to hurry along the road. About halfway back to the cabin, I noticed something sailing in the air, high above the roof of the cabin. At first I feared it was a piece of newspaper, wind-lifted from the firepit and possibly still alive with embers that might settle into and ignite the dry grass. But as I approached closer, I realized it was not a newspaper at all, but a cluster of six balloons, pink and white, that was floating over the treetops. A cluster of birthday party balloons! But where could they have come from? They were floating northeasterly from the direction of the mesa, but the nearest ranch house in that direction was Andelecio's ranch, at least six miles to the west. And since Andy goes there only occasionally, when he isn't in his family house in the village, it seemed extremely unlikely that he would be hosting a birthday party on the mesa. And if the balloons were not from Andelecio's ranch, it is maybe eighteen miles west from Begoso Canyon to the nearest settlement up on the mesa.

Anu saw the balloons, too, and watched carefully as they began to descend to the earth, not far from the road. With his indomitable puppy enthusiasm, he took off in a flash to challenge their landing but pulled back and stopped short when he recognized that

they were not the funny-shaped bird he must have thought. He abandoned the pursuit immediately and came running back to me, apparently as confused as I was. After the miles of journey these balloons had weathered, they expired in the prickles of a cholla bush a few yards from where we were standing. I put the vision in my memory box along with the other mysteries of Begoso Canyon.

But the mysteries weren't finished with me. One Sunday morning a couple of weeks later when I was driving along the wagon road on my way to the village, I had another surprise. Out in Rogelio's cow pasture, a couple of miles from the ranch, another cluster of balloons was struggling in the wind, their strings caught in the dead branches of an uprooted tree. I stopped the truck and hiked over to the tree. There were four balloons this time, these blue and white with long silver streamers tangled in the twigs. I pulled the streamers loose and the cluster rose swiftly straight up into the air, caught a strong wind current, and sailed higher and higher, out to the north over the broad Pecos Valley. I watched until they sailed so high they disappeared into the morning sun.

I can only wonder where these strange messengers could have come from, and why they should twice call on me out in this remote world.

ॐ

In the course of my life I have seen lots of rainbows. Usually they arch only halfway across the sky. A couple have been complete, but it has taken some imagination to connect both ends across a hazy midpoint. Once I even saw one of New Mexico's specialties—a double rainbow. I was walking on Guadalupe Street in downtown Santa Fe, zigzagging along the sidewalk to avoid the rain puddles, when I became aware that the people around me had stopped going wherever they were going and were standing with their faces turned up to the sky. I looked up too. Above us two parallel arcs of color sprang from the top ridge of the Sangre de Cristo Mountains east of the city and disappeared into a black cloud over our heads.

But yesterday I saw the perfect rainbow—perfect in that the spectrum of its colors lost none of its intensity as it spanned Begoso Canyon from Rowe Mesa over to the north ridge of my ranch. I say the rainbow arced from south to north, for after a few minutes it began to lose its grip on the north ridge and slowly reel itself back into the mesa until it became only a shining under the clouds, back-lighting the Nido del Aguila in a last blaze in the dark, wet air. As the light finally dissolved into the gloom of the late afternoon, a lone coyote bellowed from somewhere along the mesa cliff. I joined in with him and the two of us hollered together down the canyon.

The perfect rainbow was the final curtain call of the wildest production I have yet experienced in the canyon. I had driven out to the ranch in the early afternoon under a glowering sky, but it wasn't until I got out of my truck to unlock the last cattle gate along the wagon road that the first raindrops fell. By the time I reached the cabin a few minutes later the sky had exploded. Flashes of light shocked the air, followed within seconds by drumrolls of thunder beating against the canyon walls. Anu fled out of the truck and was jumping at the cabin door. As soon as I got the padlock off, he ran for safety under the kitchen table. I had to make two trips back to the truck to bring in food and supplies, and by then I was soaked to the skin. I fired up the woodstove in the kitchen, changed my clothes, hanging the wet ones on a viga over the stove to dry, and then huddled in the warmth of the fire to wait out the storm. Hail pounded on the tin roof with a wondrous clatter. The situation called for a cup of hot coffee, but there was no water in the cabin and I wasn't about to slosh down to the well and get soaked again. Then I realized there was no need: water was pouring out of the rain gutters at the edge of the *portal*. I put out my five-gallon plastic buckets and in a few minutes all four of them were overflowing.

The storm hammered for about two hours before the sky settled down to a soft misty rain, what the Navajo call the female rain—steady and quiet and constant. This is the rain of rainbows, and in this misty rain I had ventured out of the cabin and discovered my perfect rainbow.

When the coyote and I finished hollering, I realized there was another sound in the canyon, the sound of crashing water much louder than the patter of the gentle female rain. Of course! The Begoso must be flooding. I had never seen the Begoso run before. Although I had seen the signs of its torrential flow, I was beginning to think the Begoso was like the famous Hindu legend of the Saraswati, the river that one sees flowing only by faith. Perhaps this was my moment of faith, for the sound was definitely of a river flowing. Anu and I ran down the hill and sure enough the creek was crashing along, muddy and violent, kicking up stones from its bed, carrying the debris of the mountains downstream to the Pecos, four miles down the canyon.

Water dog that he is, and condemned to live in an arid world, Anu was in an ecstasy of wallowing. The muddy flood was too swift for swimming, and I was afraid he would be swept away. But he is young and strong and knew what he was doing. He would come out and shake—mostly all over me—then plunge back in again and out again to shake. We were both soaked, and covered with mud as well. When Anu had played enough, that is, when I decided he had played enough—I'm sure he would have been delighted to wallow for hours—we went back to the cabin, and another set of clothes was hung from the viga above the woodstove. I turned on the battery radio to hear the weather report and discovered that thirty miles away in Las Vegas, one house had been swept away, and the water on some streets of the town was four feet high.

The rain fell softly through the night, turning into a misty fog in the early morning. Sometime during the night the Begoso receded to a calm trickle of its earlier tantrum. I was glad I had brought plenty of food, for the road would be impassable now for several days.

3

One cold winter morning just before Thanksgiving, I stopped by my neighbor Seferino's house in El Pueblo to deliver some cranberry sauce I had made for his family. When I knocked at the screen door, Seferino was sitting at his kitchen table drinking coffee. He jumped up to open the door for me and offered me a cup of coffee from the pot simmering on the woodstove. He looked tired.

"I'm taking a day of rest," he said. "I've been working on my fence all week."

I did not intend to stay and visit. I was catching a cold and was in a hurry to get back to the cabin and hole up in front of the stove. But as I finished my coffee and got up to leave, Seferino stopped me.

"You must come with me to see my fence," he said. I was in no mood to go look at a barbed wire fence. Still, I didn't want to be rude to someone who was so obviously eager to show off his week's work. And he wasn't listening to my argument about catching a cold. He assured me that it would take only a few minutes for him to drive me along his fenceline.

In addition to the cow pasture south of my cabin, Seferino owns pasture land bordered by the gravel road that winds up to the top of Rowe Mesa from the paved highway along the Pecos River. This is where he had been working all week. We put Anu and his dog, Blackie, in the back of his pickup, and drove out past the last houses of the village and up the gravel road to where his fence begins.

The straight juniper posts stood upright and firm in their new holes, all of equal height, with four strands of wire stretched taut between them. The posts dipped into a gully and then advanced up a hill in perfect alignment, spaced precisely eight feet apart. It had never occurred to me that a barbed wire cattle fence could be a work of artful precision. In a section where the road runs straight, Seferino stopped the truck.

"Come and sight along the top wire," he said. I got out of the truck and went over to the fence. Carefully avoiding the barbs, I pressed my face against the wire. The fence posts merged into a solid line that arrowed up the hill. Seferino stood by the side of the road, grinning with pride.

"How did you measure it so perfectly?" I asked.

"Only with these," he laughed, tapping at his thick glasses.

I hadn't given much thought to barbed wire cattle fences before, and certainly not cattle fences as an art form. Indeed, the rusty old strands of barbed wire that surround my 240 acres in Begoso Canyon would never give rise to such a consideration. The posts wobble this way and that, consisting of whatever dead branch was at hand. They straddle the arroyos, flopping above the runoff line, hanging higher each year as rocks kick up at them and the swales grow incrementally deeper, leaving a space for the cows to poke through. So my attitude toward cattle fences was that they are a bothersome nuisance, requiring vigilance against the forces of nature, both animal and meteorological. One day when Presilino was working on the cabin, we found one of Baca's cows munching in my meadow. We chased her, and she stupidly showed us the broken wire she had found at the bottom of one of the arroyos. Presilino took his ax and cut several juniper branches to plug the gap. It has held for now, but sooner or later the runoff from a thunder shower will sweep away his Band-Aid of branches and I will have to deal with her again.

Seferino's beautiful fence reminds me of the fence the environmental artist Christo built a few years ago in Marin County, north of San Francisco. I was living in the Bay Area at the time, and the local newspapers were raving about Christo's masterpiece. I was somewhat skeptical about making a trip across the bay just to see a fence, but I was curious what the fuss was about. So I crossed the Golden Gate and drove out the Coast Highway to see for myself. As I rounded a curve high above the ocean, Christo's fence paraded before me down the soft yellow incline toward the water, the white sheets he had attached to it bulging in the ocean breeze. It was not really a fence, in that it had no divisive function. It was a celebration of line—the perfect line that rides the land, not to control it, but to define it, to make one "see" it. Of course Seferino's cattle fence has no billowing sheets, but then it didn't need sheets to announce the perfection of its linear march.

I was delighted that Seferino had overcome my objections to driving out to see his fence. I had just wanted to crawl back to my cabin and nurse my cold by the fire. But instead I was treated to a form of linear beauty I had not imagined could be created by such a seemingly humdrum event as a fenceline. From now on I will look at barbed wire fences with a different eye. I have seen the perfect cattle fence, to which I may now compare all fences.

It is indeed a strange twist of history that Seferino and I should be celebrating a barbed wire fence that closes off a piece of the San Miguel del Bado land grant. A hundred years ago such a fence would have been cut by the Hispanic vigilante group the Gorras Blancas—so named for their white caps—who terrorized anyone, Hispano or Anglo, who dared to fence off the land. Officially the backlands of the San Miguel del Bado grant had been held in common since Lorenzo Marquez and his fellow settlers had claimed them from the king in 1794. However, with the introduction of barbed wire on the western range lands in the 1880s, settlers began to fence off portions of the San Miguel grant, as well as other community grants, for their exclusive use. In July 1888 two Anglos who had settled on the San Miguel grant near what was once the village of Fulton found threatening notes on their property ordering them off the land. They refused to leave, and five months later the vigilantes struck. They cut all the fence wire, shot one of the settlers in the leg and neck, and burned down the store of the other.[2]

Over the next three years the Gorras Blancas became the scourge of San Miguel County. They expanded their operations from fence-cutting to attacks on the recently arrived Atcheson, Topeka, and Santa Fe Railroad, destroying trestles, ripping up track, and burning the ties. Railroad officials responded by refusing to buy wood for ties from San Miguel County contractors, causing severe economic hardship to the county. By 1890 the Gorras Blancas were distributing pamphlets claiming "1500 Strong and Growing Daily." It was almost impossible for territorial officials to get anyone to

testify against the group for fear of reprisals, and those who were on the outside couldn't identify the members because the attacks were always at night and the vigilantes wore masks. The few Gorras Blancas who were indicted could not be convicted because jury peers more often than not were members of the group.

The territorial governor at the time, LeBaron Bradford Prince, was confounded. The notoriety of the Gorras Blancas had spread across the nation and, according to one account, had even caused a minor blip on Wall Street, since the vigilante's activities had stopped Anglo development investment in San Miguel County. Governor Prince had been spending much of his time in Washington trying to convince Congress that New Mexico Territory was ready for statehood, and he, along with many New Mexico politicians, were afraid the destruction perpetrated by the vigilantes was ruining their chances. To add to their concerns, the purported leaders of the Gorras Blancas, Juan José Herrera and his brothers Pablo and Nicanor, had aligned themselves with the national populist party, the Knights of Labor, thus gaining a national voice for their grievances.

Emboldened by their success in driving off settlers from San Miguel County—or at least in getting rid of their fences—the vigilantes expanded their operations, cutting fences in neighboring Santa Fe and Mora Counties and on occasion striking as far away as Taos, Bernalillo, and Colfax Counties. At one point the house of the federal surveyor general was burned down.

In a list of Gorras Blancas' victims I came across in the library one day, one Julian Sandoval of San Miguel is reported as having his fences cut in July 1890. This Sandoval also owned a large orchard of some eighty trees. In one night, the Gorras Blancas chopped down every tree. Since there is only one landowner of that name in the assessor's records for San Miguel during the 1890s, he must be the same Julian Sandoval who is Andy's great-uncle and who lost his fight in the Supreme Court to preserve the common land for the settlers of the San Miguel del Bado land grant. It is curious that the man who fought his way through the levels of Anglo judiciary to the very top should be building barbed wire fences on that land.

Along with the corruption rampant in New Mexico—both governmental and private—concerning the land grants, it has been suggested that the activities of the Gorras Blancas and their political associates were a major factor pushing Congress to establish the Court of Private Land Claims in 1891.[3] By that year, however, support for the vigilantes had begun to wane. What had started as a righteous grievance against usurpers of the common lands had developed into a mayhem of property destruction and shootings. Citizens who had previously supported the movement pulled back from these excesses, as did the national Knights of Labor. Although isolated incidents continued to be reported after 1891, and some even after the turn of the century, the Gorras Blancas soon disappeared into history.

A few of the stones on which the surveyors carved the date of the first federal survey in 1902 are still in the ground at some corners of my land. Natividad built his fences between these stones. No one, other than a few errant cows, has bothered his fences in all these years.

It was perhaps inevitable that the Gorras Blancas vigilantes were riding into the night of a lost cause. The conflict between Anglos and Hispanos in San Miguel County, as in much of New Mexico, was not merely a conflict over ownership of land, but a cultural conflict over the perceived uses of the land. The Hispanic settlers valued the land insofar as it could produce and sustain; the Americans valued it primarily as an exchange commodity. The Gorras

Blancas were fighting for tradition, for the status quo, for stopping the proverbial clock. They had no plan for dealing with a future that was fast upon them. Since the arrival of the railroad, the county was becoming a major territorial commercial center. Ownership not only of the San Miguel grant but also of many other grants was in a legal limbo, and many would soon be split up. Large, mainly Anglo, cattle interests were taking over vast areas of the territory. Much as many might nostalgically yearn, and even fight, for the "way things were," the development mentality of the Anglo culture, as well as the precepts of Anglo law, had arrived in New Mexico.

How ironic, I thought as I left Seferino and drove out to Begoso Canyon, that a man whose grandfather might well have been a masked, fence-cutting vigilante should take such pride in the construction of his barbed wire fence.

4

Elizardo, the bartender at the Pueblo Bar, is always good for a story: good stories keep the customers coming back for more. So one morning when I stopped into the bar to pay for my gas and have a cup of coffee, Elizardo was ready for me with a Begoso tale.

"Do you know about the murderer who used to live out there at the top of Begoso Canyon?" he asked me, as I settled onto the bar stool.

"No, tell me," I said with anticipation. With an opening line like that, he knew he would have me in his hand.

"Back in the thirties," Elizardo began, "there was a murderer living out on the mesa above your cabin. His name was Maque

Tapia, and he and his brothers had a ranch up there in a place called Agua del Corral." I was relieved to hear that this would be a story about a murderer from a long time ago.

"Well, Maque and his brothers made their living by stealing sheep and cattle from the ranches around. They were a tough bunch, and everybody was afraid of them, especially of Maque. He was the worst. And Maque didn't just steal from the ranchers. He terrorized the villagers too. He would rob houses up and down the river. One night he crashed a dance in San Miguel—rode his horse right smack into the dance hall. He did it just to show off and scare people. Once he stole cattle from my grandfather."

"Did your grandfather ever get his cattle back?" I asked.

"Yes, he did, but he was scared to go out there alone, so he got Maque's old man who was living along the river. The two of them went out there together, and Maque's father made him give back the cattle. But my grandfather told me he was scared the whole time."

"You said he was a murderer," I said. "What happened? Did he murder one of the villagers?"

"No," Elizardo replied, "it was a Mexican national who was herding sheep up on the mesa. Maque killed him to get his sheep."

A man sitting down the bar obviously knew this story too and chimed in: "He burned the body and pushed it down an old well."

"Somehow the word got out," Elizardo continued, "and the sheriff went out to investigate and arrested Maque. They put him in the pen for ten years. Everyone breathed easier after that. But would you believe that ten years later he came back? And he started his stealing and harassing again, scaring everyone up and down the river. One day someone went out there and strangled him. Nobody knows who did it, but of course there were rumors. Whoever it was must have been pretty tough 'cause Maque was huge."

"Six-five or six-six," the man down the bar added.

"So they never caught the guy who killed him?" I asked.

Elizardo grinned at me, "Nope, and nobody looked very hard either. Everyone thought it was a good thing. If anyone really knew who did it, they never told."

I think it was a good thing too. I didn't like the idea of being the closest neighbor to a murderer, even if he would be a very old murderer by now.

Elizardo's story reminded me of another unsolved mystery in San Miguel. I asked Elizardo if he had ever heard the story of Thomas Rowland's murder some hundred and more years ago.

"No, that was a bit before my time," Elizardo laughed, "but you tell us."

"Well," I said, as Elizardo poured another round of coffee into my styrofoam cup, "I read this in a book in the library. Thomas Rowland was an adventurer who had come to New Mexico from Pennsylvania around 1830. He married a local girl and settled in San Miguel. He opened a mercantile store here and for many years traded with the wagoners who stopped at the Pecos crossing to re-stock their supplies. One night in 1858 the villagers discovered a bloody trail leading from Rowland's store. His body was found a short distance away; he had been stabbed twenty-one times."

"Gees," said the man down the bar. "Twenty-one times? Somebody really had it in for him!"

"Guess he wasn't the most popular guy in town," Elizardo said, laughing.

"Several San Miguel people were rounded up and questioned. There were rumors and insinuations of revenge or jealousy or just plain robbery—although the last scarcely accounts for the brutality of the killing. But then, just like in your story about Maque, no one was talking."[4]

"Well," said Elizardo, "people around here are pretty independent. Always have been, I guess. In the old days if someone needed killing, well somebody just took care of the problem. No need to fuss with the law. Things are different now, but life was pretty rough up to just a few years ago."

"I'll stick with the law nowadays," I said, finishing my coffee and climbing down off the bar stool. "I don't think we need any more frontier justice around here."

On one of my trips to the library I came across yet another San Miguel crime that remains a mystery—at least as to its legal outcome, since the results of the trial haven't survived. This one occurred during a fandango at the house of Ramon Lopez in the 1840s. Liquor flowed freely at these dances, sometimes with disastrous consequences. Manuel García de Lara, a lieutenant stationed at the San Miguel garrison, struck up what, according to witnesses' testimony, appeared to be a friendly conversation with Antonio Moya, a ranch-hand who worked for a wealthy landowner. In the course of their conversation, however, for some reason forever unknown, Moya insulted Lara. Lara left the dance and went outside. Moya followed after him. Suddenly Moya came staggering back into the house and collapsed on the floor, stabbed in the heart. As he was dying, he gasped out the name "Lara." Lara was accused, but claimed he hadn't done the deed. Even confronted with witnesses, he calmly denied it, claiming the witnesses were drunk and that Moya, himself, was too drunk to possibly have known who had stabbed him. Since the records are lost, we don't know the judge's verdict. But whatever it was would be beside the point. There was no doubt in the minds of the villagers as to Lara's guilt. Killing Moya was a matter of honor. After all, a lieutenant could not possibly have countenanced an insult from a mere ranchhand.[5]

Violence was a way of life on the frontier, and justice often an individual matter. San Miguel and the surrounding settlements were certainly no exception. Crime in Las Vegas, just twenty-five miles east, was notorious throughout the territory. Citizen vigilantes, imbued with a sense of social justice and fed up with what they perceived as a foot-dragging, ineffectual judicial system, determined to take charge of the administration of justice on their own. In April 1880 they published a notice in the *Daily Optic* that stated: "Las Vegas will be orderly. All thieves and murderers beware that they must behave or know the consequences, which will be the application of a hempen necktie." The notice went on to say that "the law will have to be ignored in order to speed up the process"—a threat that was peremptorily carried out on more than one occasion.[6]

The interface of cultures is almost always volatile, let alone the actions of individual criminals against their own kind. Relations between Anglos and Hispanos were often bitter, and the threat of Indian attack against both groups was persistent into the 1880s. The murderers of Rowland and Moya apparently acted out of a personal sense of justice; the activities of the vigilantes and the killing of Maque were undertaken as community improvement projects— justice for the common good, ignoring the law "in order to speed up the process."

The people of San Miguel had been accustomed to violence since the founding of the *merced*. In its early years, the village was the easternmost outpost of Spanish settlement, a buffer of protection for the capital city against the sieges of hostile Indians. Later, after the Santa Fe Trail opened, the residents frequently witnessed executions. The village was a government center during the Mexican period and after the takeover by the United States retained its position as county seat until 1864, when that function moved to the larger town of Las Vegas. Consequently, murders committed along the trail were often adjudicated in San Miguel. Convicted culprits were taken into the plaza and shot—to the questionable entertainment of the village residents.

A few days after my talk with Elizardo and his friend in the bar, I decided to hike up Begoso Canyon and then climb up the ridge to Agua del Corral to see if I could find Maque's ranch. I packed water and a lunch for myself and strapped Anu into his dog pack, filling the side bags with dog biscuits sealed in zip-lock bags and a small water bottle in each for balance. The winter morning was cold and snowless. We headed upstream and soon were into the thick brush that covers the creek as the canyon narrows. Anu was miserable. He had no sense of his own width with the dog pack filling out his sides, and the pack kept getting stuck on the bushes. So we left the canyon bottom and scrambled straight up the steep south wall of Rowe Mesa to the top. According to my USGS map, we should be at the south end of Agua del Corral. The map shows that Agua del Corral is a long, shallow drainage meandering some miles across the mesa. I hiked along the drainage for a while, hoping to find some sign of the ranch, but I couldn't find it. I didn't know where in that huge area to look.

All around me was a cold winter landscape, stretching miles into the distance in all directions. The occasional clumps of winter-dead grass gave the land a barren gray color. Here and there a straggle of windswept pine and juniper testified that life was still present. There was nothing of the color and gentleness of the river valley and creek canyons below. There is a beauty to this grim landscape, but it is a desolate, lonely beauty. And I probably wouldn't find it beautiful at all if I were dependent on it for my survival.

Perhaps the violence played out upon this land was a reflection in the human psyche of its unforgiving harshness. Men had little control over the land, the water, the weather, and hence little control over their lives. Maque's murder of the Mexican sheepherder occurred at a time when not only the was nation struggling in poverty, but the land itself was impoverished by years of drought, the same drought that drove Natividad out of his homestead. Living in Begoso Canyon—even in what must be a humble luxury compared to earlier times—I can well imagine that this dry, bleak land would breed a hardness in a people forced to claw a living from it.

The desolation of the place began to work on me. Perhaps it was just the forbidding drabness of winter or the thoughts of dark deeds past, but I found myself eager to get off the mesa. As Anu and I scrambled back down the mesa wall, Anu's pack bounced up and down as he jumped from boulder to boulder. I stopped him and took it off and carried it myself. His relief, evident in his artful bounding, was in being unencumbered; mine was in leaving the bleak mesa behind and getting back to my cabin and the familiar gentle meadows of Begoso Canyon.

5

George W. Kendall, a journalist for the *New Orleans Picayune*, wrote an account of the jubilant celebration he observed while incarcerated in a jail cell on San Miguel plaza in 1841:

> *Nothing was heard in any quarter but rejoicings and congratulations. Shouts of "Long live the Mexican Republic!" "Long live the brave General Armijo!" "Long live the laws!" and "Death to the Texans!" were heard on every side, and these were followed by discharges of musketry,*

ringing of bells, blowing of trumpets, and such music as
may be produced by cracked mandolins and rickety fiddles
when execrably played upon. A Te Deum was in the mean-
while sung in the church . . . and the guardian saint of the
place, San Miguel, with all his finery, feathers, and wings
was dragged from his resting-place to take part in the show.
Fandangos were got up in the different houses on the plaza,
and a drunken poet was staggering about singing his own
hastily made-up verses in praise of Armijo, taking his pay,
probably, in liquor—all went perfectly mad, and spent the
night in revel, riot, and rejoicing.[7]

The occasion was the celebration of the defeat of a small band of Texas soldiers by the troops of the New Mexican governor Gen. Manuel Armijo.

It was in San Miguel that Texas president Gen. Mirabeau B. Lamar's 1841 campaign to annex all of New Mexico east of the Rio Grande to the new, independent Republic of Texas fizzled to an inglorious flop. Past events that are now only stories in history books can still live on in the attitudes and suspicions—conscious or unconscious—of one group of people toward another. Especially if the event was the attempted takeover of a people's land. Although New Mexico claimed the victory in the Texas "invasion," many New Mexicans still view their Texas neighbors with a degree of suspicion—an attitude that chambers of commerce and tourist agencies are quick to deny.

Ostensibly, General Lamar's expedition was a commercial venture to increase trade between Santa Fe and Texas. But his ulterior motive, Kendall tells us, was military. Lamar believed that most New Mexicans were discontented under the yoke of Mexican rule, and he purportedly considered it his "duty" to help these oppressed people.

Fired by Lamar's belief in the New Mexicans' desire to join up with the new republic, a band of 321 soldiers set off from Austin for Santa Fe in June 1841. The *Picayune* reporter, Kendall, accompanied the expedition and later published the account of what turned out to be a disastrous fiasco—at least for the Texans. After weeks of prairie fires, Indian attacks, thirst, starvation, mutinies, and fatalities, the troops finally crossed into New Mexico, and a small scouting party of five, which included Kendall, was sent ahead toward San Miguel. The scouts were captured a few miles southeast of the village by Governor Armijo's vicious general Damasio Salazar. Salazar, pretending friendliness, tricked the party into giving over their weapons. He then proceeded to line them up to shoot them but was stopped at the last moment by a wealthy landowner of the area. In deference to the influential don, Salazar instead marched his prisoners to San Miguel, where, before continuing on to Santa Fe, they were incarcerated on the plaza for a night in what Kendall describes as "a mud hole dignified with the name of a room."[8]

The next day, Governor Armijo and his troops, marching from Santa Fe, met General Salazar and the prisoners on the road. The governor had already caught two other Texans trying to escape. They all were marched back to San Miguel and incarcerated again. This time, in order to make a point to the prisoners, Armijo had the two escapees shot in the plaza, their bodies left for the village dogs to work on. And what the dogs didn't want was tossed on a hillside for the wolves to finish.

Kendall writes that Thomas Rowland, the San Miguel merchant later to be mysteriously murdered, had been temporarily imprisoned and his goods confiscated. Governor Armijo was suspicious of Rowland and apparently assumed, even though Rowland was married to a New Mexican and had lived in San Miguel for a decade, that simply because he was an Anglo, he, too, must somehow be mixed up in this affair. Rowland was released, however, while the Texans were still in custody, and Kendall learned from the guards that he had arranged for food and blankets to be brought to the prisoners.

When news reached San Miguel that Armijo's troops had caught some of the Texas stragglers a few miles to the south—Armijo had marched fifteen hundred to two thousand troops down-river to capture some ninety starving, exhausted Texans—the village erupted into the nightlong riot of revelry that Kendall describes.

In a few days all the 180 Texans that remained of President Lamar's deluded ambitions were rounded up and assembled in the plaza at San Miguel. From there they were marched off to Mexico City, two thousand miles to the south. The treacherous Salazar was in charge of the procession as far as El Paso. In addition to robbing his prisoners of whatever valuables they still possessed and forcing them to endure almost unbearable conditions, he shot anyone who dropped behind during the freezing winter march and cut off the dead man's ears as a way of proving later that the poor straggler had not escaped. When the exhausted survivors finally arrived in El Paso, they were met by the Mexican *comandante*—and Salazar's superior—General Elias. Elias, on hearing of Salazar's insatiable avarice and cruelty, treated the Texans royally, wining and dining them. He called Salazar to account for his actions in front of his prisoner dinner guests. Salazar, confident of approval, proudly produced the cut-off ears, and Elias, disgusted, arrested him for murder. The Texans were then sent off to continue their grueling march to the Mexican capital, but without the company of General Salazar.

One final note on General Salazar: Several years later, in 1853, Salazar's son—who apparently was a chip off the old block—attacked a group of Cheyennes on the plains in an attempt to steal their horses. This caused yet another bloody Indian war in which several New Mexicans and Indians were killed. Young Salazar was also killed in the skirmish, and the old general had the gall to ask the U.S. governor in Santa Fe for five thousand dollars in compensation, arguing that it had cost quite a lot of money to rear and educate his son.[9]

Despite San Miguel's night of riotous celebration, it may be stretching rather far to call the defeat of an exhausted straggle of Texans a "victory" for New Mexico. But had things turned out differently, who knows?—maybe a good-size chunk of the Land of Enchantment might now be attached to the Lone Star State. At any rate, the insult seems to have taken deep root in the collective psyche of New Mexicans.

Today, only a few old adobes and the hulking stone and mud church that Lorenzo Marquez and his settlers built on their grant still stand intact in witness to these past events on the old plaza. In those early days, the plaza was a fortified enclosure; the church with its lookout towers was in the center. The houses were contiguous except for a few narrow alleys between them and the opening for the Santa Fe Trail from the Pecos ford. One would never know that now. There are no edges left. Scattered in among the ruins are some newer buildings, but they do not enclose a space.[10]

In the 1970s the church, the plaza, and the remaining buildings were designated on the National Register as a Historic District. But with the exception of a few restoration efforts by private owners, sufficient funds were never forthcoming to preserve what was left of the old buildings. Vandals, as well as the weather, have taken their toll. The church, however, has been in continuous use since the days of the first settlers, repaired as needed over the years by the parishioners. Aside from these few efforts, the buildings of San Miguel's history are in ruins.

In 1989 a group of historians and travel writers, including writers from the *National Geographic,* were visiting sites on the old Santa Fe Trail. They arrived in San Miguel to find a sign stating that the village was "closed." A group of residents were protesting the tour group's visit. Apparently some residents had applied unsuccessfully for grant funds to preserve and restore the plaza buildings, and they hoped to draw public attention to the sad condition of their historic village. But the protest led to nothing more than an angry exchange of letters to the editor in the Las Vegas *Daily Optic* on the propriety of picketing for preservation.[11] Today, no one in the village is certain which pile of crumbling walls was once Thomas Rowland's store, or which was the brothel, or which were the many saloons or the hotels or the "mud hole" that George Kendall described as his prison in 1841.

6

On the Sunday before Christmas I decided to brave the wintry road to the cabin and cut myself a Christmas tree. My two sons were coming for the holidays: Tonio from work in San Francisco, Rafael from school in Montana. A homegrown Christmas tree would be nicer than one from the supermarket parking lot in Santa Fe. There had been no snow for the past few days so the canyon road, though still muddy from last week's storm, should be passable. And I was eager to get back to Begoso Canyon, if only for a night.

I got up early, chased Anu into the truck, and drove out the freeway to the turnoff along the Pecos. A few minutes before nine, I passed the old church at San Miguel. The dirt parking area was already filling with the cars and pickups of the parishioners who had come from miles around to attend nine o'clock Mass. I decided to join them. I turned back and parked my truck along with the rest.

As I walked up the steps to the church, I could hear the guitars inside playing the Sunday hymns that are played in Mexico and the Hispanic churches of the Southwest. I found a seat in the back of the packed church just a moment before the guitars struck up the processional. We all stood and sang "La Guadalupana" as the priest strode down the center aisle in his embroidered chasuble, preceded by two little boys in white smocks, one of whom carried the ornate brass cross held high on its pole. As the processional hymn subsided, the boy placed the cross in its stand by the altar, and the priest turned and spoke to the congregation: "En el nombre del Padre, y del Hijo, y del Espíritu Santo." We all murmured "Amen" as he signed us with his blessing.

As is the custom in many New Mexico churches, the celebration here in San Miguel is spoken in both Spanish and English. The priest, if he is a Hispano, moves with admirable bilingual skill from one language to the other. If he is an Anglo, he'll do his best. I am always impressed and envious of the ability of Spanish New Mexicans to chatter along in both languages without a trace of accent affecting either. Only the English of older people still has a tinge to it, and by now only those over perhaps eighty don't speak English at all.

The readings for this Fourth Sunday of Advent were from the prophet Micah: "You, Bethlehem-Ephrathah. . . . From you shall come forth for me one who is to be ruler in Israel"; and from the letter to the Hebrews: "On coming into the world Jesus said: '. . . As is written of me in the book, I have come to do your will, O God.'"

The congregation sang the Hallelujah, and the priest stepped forward to read the passage from the Gospel of Luke in which Mary goes to greet her cousin Elizabeth, and Elizabeth's baby "leapt in her womb" in acknowledgment of Mary's greeting. Then the priest spoke to the assembled about the importance of the words we use for greetings and why in Spanish one says "buenos días"—good days—instead of just "good day"—that is, in Spanish we ask God to give our friends many good days, unlike in English, where we offer them just one. There seemed to be a subtle suggestion of disapproval of those parsimonious speakers of English who offer their friends only a single good day.

After the people had filed down the aisle to accept the body and blood of the Eucharist, the priest announced that the Mass was ended and the congregation answered "Demos gracias a Dios." I took the church bulletin from the sexton on my way out the door and put it in my purse along with the Sunday paper I had picked up in my driveway when I started out from Santa Fe. I planned to read them both when I got out to the ranch. I also stopped in the little community building adjacent to the church and bought a lemon pie at the youth group's bake sale to take with me.

The day was sunny and unseasonably warm for December. Anu ran the four miles of dirt road alongside the truck, stopping to rest as I got out to open the cattle gates. When we reached the cabin I fixed a late breakfast for both of us—lemon pie and coffee for me, kibble and pie crumbs for Anu. I planned to spend only one night since I had to be back in town the next day. But the purpose of this trip was to cut a Christmas tree. I took the ax and started out across the wintry meadow, looking for the perfect symmetrical piñon pine. Anu raced ahead of me, joyous to be free of the city. I walked about a quarter mile before I spotted my tree jutting out from the steep bank above Begoso Creek. Whacking an ax at a live tree, especially one in such an awkward position, is a lot harder than splitting dry firewood, but I finally felled it and dragged it up to the road to pick up later with the truck. My mission accomplished, we walked back to the cabin, and I settled into the sunshine to read the Sunday paper. Anu sat next to me and chewed on the same old dry elk horn he'd been working on for months.

The news was the usual unnerving reports of burglaries, political cat fights, and car crashes. I soon tossed the paper into the stack by the woodpile and picked up the church bulletin. I found the doings of San Miguel parish far more settling. Then my eye caught a heading for "posadas." The posada is a Christmas custom of Mexico and Hispanic areas of the Southwest. The people of a village or neighborhood go from house to house enacting the search of Mary and Joseph to find shelter. The article announced that there would be three posadas this week, one in the village of Bernal, one in Lagunita, and to my delight, one that evening in El Pueblo, the nearest village to my land. The posada was to begin at seven o'clock. I decided that rather than spend the night at the cabin, I would drive down later to the village, go to the posada, and then return to Santa Fe afterward.

By five o'clock the sun was down and the evening was cold. I didn't want to bother to fire up the woodstove just for a short time, so I decided to leave early and stop by Seferino's rambling adobe at the Pueblo gate and visit for an hour. I stopped along the road to pick up my tree and then drove on down the canyon. Luckily Seferino was at home. He had just returned from Andelecio's house with a jug of homemade wine. Seferino said he wasn't going to the posada, so after warming myself by his woodstove and sharing a couple of glasses of Andy's heady wine, I left and drove the half mile up the road to the tiny pink-painted mission church of San Antonio de Padua in Upper Pueblo. I parked up on the road, leaving Anu in charge of our Christmas tree, and walked down the dirt lane leading to the little church. The posada was to start with a Mass, so I was in for another round of scripture and ritual.

I had never been in this church before, because it isn't used on a regular basis. Once I tried to peek in the windows, but like the windows of my cabin, they were covered with lace curtains and I couldn't see in. But tonight the little church was blazing with lights, and cars were parked up and down the road. The church held perhaps a hundred people, counting the many packed against the walls. Since there were no seats left on the main floor, I climbed up the narrow staircase to the loft, and the people there squeezed together to make room for me on one of the long benches. The ceiling over the loft was so low we had to dodge a large viga whenever we stood up. To the left of the altar four men were playing guitars and singing Spanish carols. Two Christmas trees, wrapped round with strings of lights, stood behind the altar under the plaster statue of San Antonio perched high on the wall. The trees were topped with coronas of bulbs that flashed on and off behind the priest's head all during the Mass.

After the priest had given us his final blessing and wished us a Merry Christmas in both English and Spanish, he suggested we all might chip in to cover the cost of the heating bill for the little church, and two men passed around the collection baskets. Then the congregation filed out into the cold night, we of the loft waiting till everyone else had left in order to descend the steep and slightly rickety wooden steps.

Outside, the four men with the guitars were strumming carols and the crowd was milling around. After a few minutes, a donkey appeared out of the night carrying a little dark-eyed girl of about ten years dressed in a white shawl that covered her hair. The donkey's halter was held by a young man, draped to the shoulders in a colorful burnoose held in place by a rolled band around the crown of his head: Mary and Joseph had arrived and the posada was on.

Slowly the people moved into a loose formation behind the players, who walked behind Mary and Joseph and the donkey. We walked along the dirt lane singing carols until we came to our first house. Then the guitarists stepped forward to the door and began to sing the traditional posada song, which asks for lodging for a poor carpenter and his pregnant wife: "En nombre del cielo, os pido posada." The door of the house opened, and from inside the petition was answered by singers who stated in verse quite flatly to move on: "Aquí no es mesón: Sigan adelante." And the door was closed on us. Joseph led the donkey away from the house, and we proceeded behind them, moving slowly up to the highway, walking and singing along with the guitars until we came to the next house. Here the same petition was offered in verse as before, and again, after the exchange with the singers behind the half-open door, we were rejected.

The December night was cold but clear, with a moon just slightly on the wane. Along the road we passed houses strung with Christmas lights from the rooftops down to the ground. A score of children walked with us, bundled as we were in down jackets, scarves, and mittens. We walked about a quarter mile in the moonlight, singing. There was scarcely any traffic on the winding two-lane road. We moved over to let one car pass, and the only other one we encountered drove along behind us and become part of the procession. As we approached the cluster of buildings that form the village of Lower Pueblo, people came out of their houses to sing with us. We stopped at another house, and the same petition was repeated. The door of this house, too, was closed on us.

Finally we came to the long low community building that faces the highway directly across from the Pueblo Bar. The bar emptied

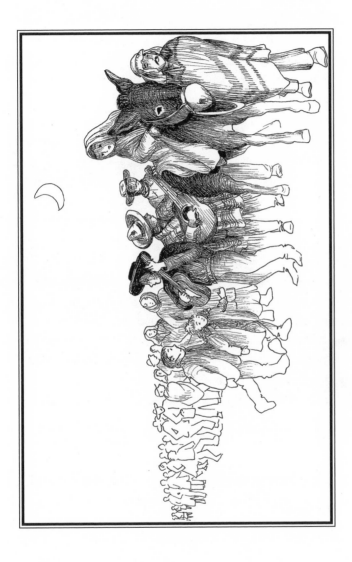

out at our approach, and its patrons crossed the road to join us. By now our group had swollen to well over a hundred. We approached the door of the building and began our song. The door opened a crack, and from inside we were answered in verse as before. But this time the exchange sounded more hopeful: "Dichosa la casa que alberga este día / a la Virgen pura, la hermosa María. Entren santos peregrinos!" And the door was flung open to welcome us.

The building was very old, built of adobe with huge log vigas spanning the ceiling. The room was warm after our cold walk, and we quickly shed our mittens and scarves. Christmas lights and boughs of greenery were strung along the walls. There was a fireplace at one end and tables and chairs were set up in long rows. Along one wall was a magnificent spread. Pots of green chile stew and posole, steamed tamales and meat cooked with hot red chile, pans of enchiladas baked with chicken and cheese, trays of sliced turkey and ham, tortillas and breads, bowls of salad, coffee and punch, and every kind of dessert. Three women stood behind the food table, ready to serve us. The priest, who had accompanied us on our pilgrimage, was invited to head the food line. Slowly, over the next hour or so, the crowd worked its way up to the food table, and the women fed all hundred and more of us.

When my turn came and I had filled my plate with all it could hold, I went to sit at one of the long tables. I didn't know anyone at the posada; the few people I had met in the village were not there. After a while, however, one of the guitarists came over and greeted me in English. I hadn't heard a word in English since the bilingual Mass earlier in the evening. I recognized my neighbor Gabriel, who pastures his cows just beyond my property. He had stopped by the cabin one day last spring to welcome me to my new home. I asked him to join me, and we talked for a time about the village and the people and the posada. He told me there had been three posadas in the valley the week before, but tonight everyone agreed that ours was the best. We almost had to shout at each other over the babble of voices and the scampering of children running back and forth to the dessert table for seconds and thirds of cake and biscochitos, Jell-O and punch.

When the celebration was over, my neighbor gave me a ride back to my truck. My tree was still there, and Anu greeted me with a look of offended boredom. I rewarded his patience with two biscochitos I had slipped into my pocket for him from the feast table.

As I drove back to Santa Fe in the late night with my Christmas tree rustling in the wind in the back of my truck, the moon highlighted the strata of ancient seas on the escarpment of Rowe Mesa above the road. I felt I was driving away from another country, from another time. From a world where one has no way of knowing what to expect from one hour to the next. I had driven down this same highway early in the morning with nothing planned but to chop down a Christmas tree and then settle into the cabin for the night. And then I had found myself walking down a moonlit highway with Mary, Joseph, a donkey, and a crowd of villagers seeking a place to give birth to the Christ Child—and finding it in the welcome and bounty of a village feast.

7

I awoke early one January morning to find myself snowed in. Not snowed in as in Jack London stories of Yukon cabins, where only the stovepipe sticks up above the drifts, but snowed in as far as any possibility of driving my light pickup out of the canyon. Not that I was planning to. I didn't have to be back in Santa Fe for several days, and I had covered myself by calling in town before I came out here to say that if I didn't show up, it would be because I couldn't get out. There was a pot of beans from the night before sitting on the cold cookstove and plenty of cans of soup; still a half cord of wood under the *portal,* three gallons of kerosene in the storeroom, and a shelf of books. The dog food supply was a little low, but Anu would prefer to share my beans anyway.

My Toyota hulked like a sleeping polar bear out by the fence gate, and the road was a ribbon of unsullied silver snaking through the meadow. I could tell the road from the meadow only by the tips of the yellow weeds that stop at the road edge. The ten or so inches of snow that had fallen in the night had turned the escarpment of Rowe Mesa into a wall of white above the canyon, and the dark branches of the piñons were sagging with heavy puffs. Anu danced around the cabin with excitement, intent on convincing me we must go for a hike. I made him wait while I fired up the stove for coffee and bundled myself in snow boots, mittens, and parka.

The drifts were deep along the edges of the canyon, so I kept to the road for our walk. Anu raced in circles out in the meadow, then shot ahead of me, turning to race back at me at full speed. I had to dodge his assaults not to end up sprawled in the snow. His ecstacy was catching; I threw snowballs at him and he jumped to catch them in his mouth. The game seemed to add, if possible, to his joy; it certainly increased the force of his headlong attacks.

In the meadow, the prickly spires of the yuccas fanned up from the snow in clusters like cold white porcupines. The cloud cover hovered low at the rim of the mesa, a pearly ceiling alive with light from the invisible sun above, sealing me into the canyon.

I didn't want the fire to go out in the stove, so after half an

hour I turned and started back toward the cabin. Anu tried to dis-
suade me with a couple more assaults but gave up, disappointed,
and trotted back by my side. I was surprised to hear the sound of a
heavy motor in the distance. Someone was driving the road behind
me. Soon Andrés, one of the Baca brothers, caught up with me, his
heavy truck loaded with alfalfa he was bringing out to his cold cows
weathering in the fields beyond my cabin. Andrés offered me a ride,
but the morning world was too lovely to ride. I told him to stop by
for coffee on his way back.

He did. As we were drinking coffee in the warm cabin, he suggested a business deal with me.

"How about leasing your meadow to me for a month?" he
asked. "My cows are really hungry and your grass hasn't been grazed
for years. It would be good to let them cut it back." I certainly didn't
want my meadow overgrazed like the lands around me, but a month
of cows might be a good idea, along with all that natural fertilizer.
I told him I would think about it and would let him know next week.

When I drove out to the canyon a week later, there was no
sign of the snow. Only damp, muddy earth everywhere. I had no
sooner got the stoves going when I heard Andrés's truck pull up at
the fence gate.

"Hello," he called from the cab window as I walked out to
meet him. "What about the cows?"

We agreed he would bring them—twenty-seven cows with
ten calves and more on the way. In return for the month of grass, he
would bring me a cord of stove-length fire wood.

A few days later I awoke to the sounds of shouting and honking and mooing. Three pickup trucks were herding a bunch of very
annoyed mothers through the narrow gate behind my cabin. I went
out to watch, and soon my meadow was dotted with cows, many of

which had small brown bodies glued to their undersides. Anu was wild with excitement at the sight. I was afraid he might try to chase them, but after a couple of enthusiastic passes, he quickly backed off in the face of fierce maternal glaring. By the cabin gate was a big pile of wood Andrés had dumped there the night before. I spent the morning stacking the logs under the *portal* to keep them out of the snow that I knew would be back again soon.

Cattle-grazing on the San Miguel grant—as in much of northern New Mexico—is more an occupation of love and Hispanic cultural tradition than an economically profitable enterprise. The land is rugged and arid and the grass is sparse. Most of these small-scale operations entail caring for about twenty cows on fifteen to twenty acres of grazing land per cow. Perhaps 60 percent of the cows will produce calves in a year. If the market is good one year and the calves are healthy and big, one might get a dollar a pound in Las Vegas or Belen for a four-hundred-pound calf. But of course one might get less. Andrés got seventeen calves this year from the twenty-seven cows that shared my meadow for a month, but coyotes made off with two of them.

This kind of husbandry doesn't bring much to the family table. Most of my neighbors have other jobs or are retired, and the cattle are just a supplementary source of income. The labor of herding them from one pasture to another or up onto the mesa to government-leased land, or fixing broken fences and trampled watering holes, or hauling out extra feed in the winter is a "spare time" expense that cannot be counted.

Nevertheless there are noneconomic rewards for all this labor. For many rural Hispanic families, cattle-raising is a way of life—a cultural tradition that has tied them to the land for generations. It keeps the kids busy and out of trouble and provides older people with a retirement job. It produces meat for the household and is often seen as a kind of savings account. If things get bad, one can always sell a cow.

One day, when I stopped at the Pueblo Bar in the village to buy gas and catch up on the latest gossip, the talk was of my neighbor Seferino.

"He's become a mother," Elizardo, the bartender, laughed. "He is raising a little calf he found starving up on the mesa, and the calf is following him around wherever he goes."

I went over to Seferino's house to see for myself. As I drove into the yard, a little chestnut calf was sucking on a huge white plastic nipple that stuck out of a bright blue nursing bucket tied to a fence post. He didn't bother to stop sucking or even look at me when I walked up to him. Seferino came out of the house. He looked slightly harassed.

"He won't let me alone, " he said. "Every time I walk out of the house, he starts following me around. He thinks I'm his mother!"

I asked Seferino how he had come by his new baby.

"I found the mother up on the mesa," he said. "She had got herself wedged between two huge rocks and was dead. This little guy was starving, barely alive. So I brought him home."

The baby calf looked quite healthy and contented to me. "Will you keep him?" I asked.

"Oh yes, I'll keep him for a while, anyway. His name is Fito."

Fito left his nursing bucket and came over to butt his head affectionately against his new mother. I wonder what Seferino will do if Fito keeps up such touching demonstrations of love when he grows up to be a big happy bull.

Living in the backlands of the old San Miguel *merced* for the past several months certainly brought out the history buff in me. I spent hours in the library and the church and state archives sleuthing through the events that occurred in New Mexican territory that specifically affected San Miguel: the Spanish grant to the early settlers, the Indian wars, the opening of the trail, the Texas Expedition, General Kearny's takeover and the Treaty of Guadalupe Hidalgo, the coming of the railroad, the loss of the *merced* to the new government, and the subsequent decline of the villages. These are all well-documented, and it didn't take long for me to piece together the rise and fall of San Miguel del Bado.

Putting people into these occurrences was more difficult. Historians tend to deal with judicial or political events—wars, treaties, documents—and the political and military honchos who are involved in these events. The common people of a village are seldom heard from, unless they act in some collective, revolutionary manner. Hence it is difficult to discover much about the daily life of such people. I was curious to know something about the ancestors of the *merced:* what kind of people they were and how they lived. Even trying to piece together the relatively recent world of Natividad from the stories of the few people who remember him and the testimonies of his droppings is difficult.

But now and then I would come across some clues about life on the *merced.* For example, in a book about public health in New Mexico, I came across the story of Julianita Baca. I don't know if her early life was typical, but it does offer some insight into nineteenth-century life in San Miguel, especially the life of a woman.[12]

Julianita was born around 1843 in the village of Chaparito, several miles southeast of the town of Las Vegas. When she was twelve years old, her parents arranged for her to marry a man she had never met. The child moved with her new husband to San Miguel del Bado. Julianita's husband was a *cibolero*, a buffalo hunter. When he went out on the prairies to hunt, he would be gone from the village sometimes for months. In his absence, Julianita was subjected to an angry mother-in-law, who had little patience with her new daughter's childish ways, one day taking the girl's doll away and burning it. On his return from one of his expeditions, Julianita's husband presented his young wife with an iron stove, said to be the first in the village. It took her some time to get up the nerve to use it; she was afraid it would melt.

Perhaps it is a statement of health conditions at the time that of Julianita's twenty-five babies, including three sets of twins, only four survived. During one of her pregnancies, she became extremely ill and promised God that if she recovered, she would become a *medica*, a healer, so she could help other people. She did recover, and made good her promise. Along with the prayers and novenas she offered up for her patients, she learned the curative powers of local herbs. She was especially adept at treating rheumatism with the use of the herb *hediondilla*, a most vile-smelling weed, a form of creosote bush. Her fame as a healer quickly spread. So successful were her cures that people came to San Miguel from all over New Mexico and from neighboring states as well. She continued healing others until her death in 1948 at the age of 105. Julianita's story was related by her granddaughter; the Baca house still stands on the plaza opposite the church.

In general, however, the journals of the traders and soldiers and all-around adventurers who followed the Santa Fe Trail were my best source of descriptions of the village and the people, although often one must read beyond the obvious cultural bias of the writers.

The earliest description of San Miguel that I came across was that of Col. Meredith M. Marmaduke, who accompanied William Becknell's third trading venture along the trail in 1824: "A description of the place can best be given by comparing it to a large brick yard, where there are a number of kilns put up and not burnt, as all the houses are made of bricks dried in the sun. . . . All the roofs are entirely flat. The inhabitants appear to me to be a miserably poor people, but perfectly happy and contented." [13]

Some twenty-two years later the scene had apparently not changed much. The Mormon Battalion leader John D. Lee, however, had little good to say about the people:

Passed through St. Magill (a Spanish town) about 11. . . .
Their ploughs are made entirely of wood yet not resembling
any thing I ever before saw. In this village is a regular built
Catholic Chappel & the only resemblance that I saw was
the cross on one of the cupeloes—as there was one on each
corner facing the East. All buildings here are built of un-
tempered mourtars. Arround the chapel, the Priest residence,
& some of the Public houses were enclosed by mud walls
from 10 to 12 feet high—their Pounds or enclosures for their
stock, when penned are built in like manner—There is cer-
tainly less enterprise, industry, or economy manifestd among
these beings than any others, who pretend at all to civiliza-

tion. . . . When ever we would hault near their settlements (as they all settle in villages) our lines would be filled with them coming to trade . . . their principle trafic to travelers is corn (which in their tongue is Mice)—onions Peper, Squashes, whiskey, apples & mellons & in fact they will trade any thing they have. . . . at 5 we encamped at one of their settlements at a beautiful stream of water 1 mi North of the road. Evening clear & cool.[14]

One might suggest that this sour Mormon could use some orthography lessons. Colonel Marmaduke found the people "perfectly happy and contented," whereas Lee comments in his journal that they are "dark, swarthy, dirty, lazy, filthy, indolent, raged & naked, uncivilized, miserable looking beings."[15]

These accounts chronicle the writers' encounters with a people who had been culturally and geographically isolated from their European origins, perhaps for some families as many as 250 years. New Mexico had little contact with either of the countries that had claimed sovereignty over her. To the villagers, Spain was probably little more than a legend. At the beginning of the nineteenth century, the Spanish king was much too busy trying to protect the homeland from threatened invasion by Napoleon to be concerned about the fringes of an already shaky empire. As for Mexico, it was a ten-week trip across vast desert just to get to Chihuahua, let alone the months it took to get to Mexico City and back. The territory was cut off from the United States to the east by mountains and prairies and from Spanish settlements in Arizona and California by the same. The settlers were, in a sense, imprisoned by the presence of hostile, nomadic Indians. And the villages were isolated from each other. A few wealthy individuals of Santa Fe or Taos were able to travel out of the area, and some sent their children to schools in the United States. But up until the opening of the trail, what little intercultural contact the impoverished villagers had was primarily with the more or less friendly Pueblo Indians. They had little to do with the government in Santa Fe or with the *ricos* who would soon be further enriching themselves on the trail trade. And with Mexico's expulsion of the Spanish-born priests in 1826, the villagers lost access to the limited opportunities for learning that the Franciscans had provided. It is interesting to note that while the villages that developed on the land grants were expected to make provisions for a church, there was no such requirement for a school.

Learning much from the Indians, the settlers developed ways to survive in a difficult environment. Their society was based strongly on custom and tradition, tightly bound by the ties of family, community, and religion. It is unfortunate that of the traders and others who finally penetrated the area in the first half of the nineteenth century, few if any were "anthropologically" sensitive. Much more could have been learned about these villagers and their adjustment to their environment at the time of contact than the brief descriptions in the surviving journals. Still, these descriptions, when we read beyond the cultural bias, provide much of what we do know about the villagers in those early days.

The San Miguel women come in for special praise from the trail travelers, as well as some ridicule. George Kendall, the Louisiana reporter incarcerated on the San Miguel plaza in 1841 along with the ill-fated Texans, is especially taken with the women: "We were visited by every girl in the town, and from the ranchos in the vicinity. Each time they brought us some little delicacy to eat: if ever men came near being killed with kindness, we were the victims." Kendall finds the women "joyous, sociable, kind-hearted creatures almost universally, liberal to a fault, easy and naturally graceful in their manners." However, he doesn't think much of their makeup: "The faces of the majority of the girls [are] stained, either with vermilion or the juice of some red berry, and many of them presenting a truly hideous appearance." Matt Field, like Kendall a reporter for the *New Orleans Picayune,* writing a couple of years before Kendall, is also impressed by the San Miguel girls. He finds them beautiful, but he wishes they would wash their faces: "the simple señoritas are very fond of vermilion, and they daub it on forehead and nose as well as on the cheeks, showing that their ideas of beauty are in some measure derived from the Indians." [16]

Praise of women does not come only from the men. Susan Magoffin, one of the first Anglo women to travel the trail, gives us her impression of the San Miguel women in her 1846 journal:

> *I did think the Mexicans were as void of refinement, judgement &c. as the dumb animals till I heard one of them say "bonita muchachita"! And now I have reason and certainly a good one for changing my opinion: they are certainly a very quick and intelligent people. Many of the mujeres came to the carriage, shook hands and talked with me. One of them brought some tortillas, new goat's milk, and stewed kid's meat with onions. . . . They are decidedly polite, easy in their manners, perfectly free &c.* [17]

How easily a little kindness changed this woman's preconceived attitude toward a people as being "as void of refinement as the dumb animals" to being "a very quick and intelligent people"!

Clearly there is an openness on the part of this observer and a kindness here that the Mormon John Lee—later convicted and executed for his part in the Mormon Meadow Mountain massacre—is too bigoted to experience. Yet these brief impressions of "outsiders" don't tell us much, except perhaps about the person writing them.

San Miguel did have its revolutionary moment of rebellion, although it fizzled before anyone in the village got into trouble. A few months after the U.S. takeover, the San Miguel priest, Father Leyba, along with his friend Father Antonio Martinez, in Taos, was involved in the abortive attempt by a group of patriots to throw out the invaders and install Tomás Ortiz, the former alcalde of Santa Fe, as governor. These men were disgusted that Governor Armijo had simply handed the province over to the Americans in 1846 and fled. General Kearny had moved on to take California. The governor he left in charge, Charles Bent, was murdered by the rebels in Taos. Father Leyba tried to rouse the revolutionary fervor of his San Miguel parishioners, but apparently they had no stomach for the fight. The Americans quickly quashed the rebellion.

The underlying current of disdain and even contempt for New Mexicans and their culture that we read in some of these excerpts runs throughout the comments of the Anglos in their confrontations with Hispanics. And with the exception of a certain deference to the Santa Fe *ricos* with whom they hobnobbed, the Americans' attitude of contempt for their new citizens was shared by many in Washington as well. The no-doubt apocryphal story goes that Gen. William Tecumseh Sherman suggested that the United States might do well to declare war on Mexico all over again and force it to take back New Mexico.[18]

The state of illiteracy in the newly acquired territory may have been appalling, given the former government's neglect of the area and the resistance of the Mexican Church to popular education, still the U.S. Congress didn't bother to appropriate money for public schools in New Mexico for years. What schools there were were run by religious groups. The poorer people in San Miguel didn't have much time for schooling: time spent in school would be time away from the business of survival.

One account I came across describes the childhood of boys in San Miguel in the nineteenth century: Early in the spring the boys were taken out to open range, where they remained until the fall, guarding the sheep and goats and cattle. The family sent out staples once a month. The boys, armed with a _boladora_, a type of slingshot, and a bow and arrows could provide their own supper. These boys were often killed or stolen by Indians.[19]

Not until the 1890s did public education become mandatory in the territory. Mandatory for some, perhaps, but apparently not for the likes of Natividad, whose signatory _X_ I have on the deed to the Begoso property. Of course the Civil War and its aftermath intervened in domestic development for some time after the takeover. Perhaps the only reason New Mexicans sided with the Union was that, despite the disdain in which they were held and the lack of concern in Washington for their social and economic development, the people hated the Texans more than they hated their U.S. conquerors. If the South won the war, New Mexico would probably be taken over by the Texans. Anything seemed better than that.

But contempt breeds contempt in return. And the attitudes of mutual antagonism nursed in these times of 150 years ago, along with the frontier lawlessness and violence that left both the Indians and the Hispanos bitter with the sense of injustice, still today challenge the conscience of New Mexicans of all origins.

9

"Haven't seen anything like this in all my sixty-five years," my neighbor Tadocio said to me as we walked along his mud-dry acequia. "It's incredible. I can't put my corn and squash in this year, and at this rate, I just don't know if I can afford to keep my cows any longer. Joe said I could use his pasture, but there's not much grass up there and what am I supposed to do for water?"

It is already May. There has been no rain in New Mexico for weeks, and last winter the snow was light. Heavy rain doesn't come until July, but usually there are late snows and rain in April and May to revive the chewed-down grass. But not this year. The grass still shows no signs of greening and the ranchers have to buy hay, which is also in short supply. Last year hay was $2.75 a bale and now it's up to $4.00 and rising. Out at my cabin, Natividad's rock-lined well still has water, but it is muddy and low. I use it just for washing dishes and have been hauling drinking water out from town in five-gallon gasoline cans.

Everyone I talk to voices the same lament: How can we keep our cows? At two to three hay bales each a week, it's costing more to feed them than they're worth. To make matters worse, there's a surplus of beef on the market and prices are abysmal. One neighbor sold three pairs—a cow with calf—in Las Vegas last week for $725, the price he would have got for a single pair in a good year.

And then there are the fires. Not near us—yet—but higher in the mountains. We can see the columns of smoke rising on the far ridges. The seventeen-thousand-acre Los Alamos fire has blanketed the sky over Santa Fe with an eerie murk for a week, the sun shining through as a dirty orange ball. There is a feeling of impending doom in the air, a strange foreboding, rather like during a full eclipse, and the dogs start barking. I haven't dared to build a fire in my firepit or even light the woodstoves. My neighbor Gabriel tells me he caught a couple of boys playing with matches and chewed them out good. When they gave him some lip about it, he set the county fire marshal on them.

This year's drought has brought stories of how wet the weather used to be. Andelecio remembers that Begoso Creek would run continuously for two months every spring. And others tell me that their grandfathers would talk about the wonderful pastures and abundant water. Indeed, New Mexico weather has changed, in that it goes through cycles of wet and dry, and at present we are in a dry period. However the landscape itself has changed dramatically, and the weather is not the main cause of this change.

Back in 1885 a promotional pamphlet for San Miguel County prepared for the New Orleans World Exposition boasts of the good winter range, where no extra feeding is necessary, and of the successful sheep and cattle industries based on the quality of the grass and the well-watered pasture lands. The pamphlet goes on to say that Las Vegas was the largest wool market in the territory and the county cattle count was three hundred thousand. The lumber industry comes in for praise as well: In 1883–84 alone, one thousand train cars shipped 10 million board feet of timber, along with hundreds of thousands of railroad ties cut in the mountains. Indeed I can see clearly from my cabin the long chute running down the escarpment of Bernal Mesa where the logs were pushed over the edge to the valley below. The scar hasn't healed in more than a hundred years.[20]

The World Expo pamphlet was overly optimistic about the future of ranching and logging in San Miguel County. The change from subsistence farming to a cash economy in the last years of the century caused a devastation to the land from which it has not recovered. Massive logging in the mountains with no thought to reforestation, along with years of fire suppression, have changed the nature of the forests, causing the growth of understory far more susceptible to fire. Additionally, the destructive overgrazing and soil compaction by the trampling of animal hooves on the foothills and plains have destroyed the native vegetation and turned the land into a network of gullies that was never there before. The gullies score the slopes in deep gashes, as if made by a great knife slashing through the soil, twisting in the wounds to increase the agony. They drain off the denuded topsoil and lower the water table, leaving little behind for the growth of grasses. Hence when a wet year does come along and the streams are full to overflowing, we are witnessing the inability of the soil to absorb the runoff, rather than a testimony to a water-rich landscape.

Still, biologists tell us from tree ring data that, with the exception of certain periods, New Mexico weather cycles are not much different now from in the past, and the fires and loss of pasture land are the result of human actions rather than the weather. Unfortunately many of the ranchers are still overgrazing the land, and when we get a bad year like this one, it is easier for them to blame the weather than their stock-raising practices for their misfortunes.

I hear in my neighbors' laments about the drought the worry that if the weather continues in this hot, dry cycle, it may mean the end to a traditional way of life that has survived, but barely, in the Hispanic villages of northern New Mexico. As one of my neighbors, Celedonio, puts it: "I remember back in the fifties my folks went through a drought like this. But they had no choices. Cattle-raising was their only source of income, and they just had to struggle through. Most of us these days have other jobs, and the cows are more of a family tradition than a way to make a living."

Last week the villagers took the statue of San Antonio out of the little church at El Pueblo and carried him around the village to pray for rain. However, Saint Anthony is not known for his powers over the weather, and the heavens have not—as yet, anyway—complied with his petition.

And now it is June and the drought continues. For the last few days thunderheads have risen for a few hours over the Sangre de Cristos to the north, but they dissipate, taking their precious water with them, leaving the sky blue and clear by late afternoon. Yesterday when I stopped at the Pueblo Bar for gas, there was talk of nothing but drought. One of the villagers had sold all his cows in Belen, bringing scarcely $150 a cow, and only $800 for his prime bull.

"The big ranchers with lots of land are really raking it in at the auctions," growled one of the regulars from his bar stool. "Yea, they're gettin' them cows for a third the usual price," said another. "And did you see in the paper that the government is talkin' about importin' beef from Chile? Now why in hell would they do that?"

Having no answer to this rhetorical question, I paid Elizardo for the gas and drove out to the cabin in the late warm sunshine. Not a cloud in the sky.

☙

Early this morning Anu and I climb the south ridge on the shoulder of Rowe Mesa. As we cross through the meadow, the yellow tufts of dry straw grass crackle under foot, and Anu snorts to free his nose of the iron-red dust. We climb for half an hour till we enter the cool ponderosa forest on the slope of the mesa. From this height I can see Pecos Baldy and the perfect cylindrical cone of Barillos Peak north across the Pecos Valley. And to the east, the top of Starvation Peak, a sheer-sided, flat-topped butte carved into a magnificent monument by millennia of wind and rain.

The first time I saw Starvation Peak rising above the freeway some fifteen miles west of Las Vegas, I was sure that such a striking geologic formation was bound to have a legend wrapped around its precipitous walls. And as one might guess from its name, Starvation Peak does have a story. I came across it in a pamphlet of legends of the Upper Pecos:

> *In the early 1800s, a group of Spanish families from San Miguel del Bado were herding sheep on the broad meadows southeast of Starvation Peak. This was Apache land, but the nomadic Indians had not been there for some time, and the people thought it would be safe to let their sheep graze there. One day, however, a large band of Apaches was spotted riding toward the meadows. The frightened Spaniards, too far from San Miguel to make it back to the safety of the village, had no choice but to climb up the steep walls of the peak. At least they thought they could ward off an attack from the top. But the Indians didn't attack. Instead they camped at the foot, surrounding the base and cutting off all escape. And waited. After three days, the families ran out of food and water. But the Indians didn't move. Finally, on the fourth night, one of the hostages managed to creep un-*

seen down the slope and sneak past the campfires while the
Indians were busy eating their dinner. He walked through
the night to alert the garrison at San Miguel. The next
morning the Indians were scattered by the guns of the sol-
diers. The starving Spaniards were saved, but not without
the loss of some who died on the peak.[21]

The heat of the day is beginning to capture us even here in the forest. I dig Anu's cup out of my pack and give him a drink of the water I've carried up the ridge. And then we climb down into one of the many arroyos that drains the mesa above us. A stand of cottonwoods, fresh with new leaves, lines the edge of our arroyo. Their feet dig down into the sandy embankment, nursing from some deep source of moisture that has eluded the thin-rooted grasses. The brilliant chartreuse leaves are a stark shout of color against the muted dark curtain of piñon and juniper. Our path is interrupted by stone ledges, which in a storm drop gushing waterfalls into broad pools below them. But there is no water now, not even mud. In one of the dry pools, a bear has left his scat. Perhaps he was hoping to find water; he must be as disappointed as I am. At the foot of the slope, where the arroyo widens to join the Begoso, I gasp at the stench of putrefying flesh. A half-eaten cow is rotting in the hot sun on the Baca's side of the fence. One less cow to take to auction.

It was such a drought as this that drove Natividad out of Begoso Canyon during the depression. At the turn of the century, when he homesteaded this land, the weather was wet. But by the 1930s, he could no longer dry farm his corn and beans. His well is almost dry now. The bucket sits on the bottom, and I have to tip it to bring up a bucketful of silt. It's easy enough for me to drive into

town and fill up my gas cans with water, but that water is only for drinking. No one can farm here anymore.

☙

At last, for the past week, the rains have come. I awoke from a nap this hot July afternoon to the delicious clatter of hail raining down like gravel on the tin roof of the cabin. Not that the drought is over. The Santa Fe weather reports warned us in June that there was only enough water in the city reservoir to last through this month. Now with the rains, they tell us that ten days have been added to the countdown.

But here in Begoso Canyon the grass is beginning to tuft green again under the dead straw, and the water in my well is up above the muck line where it had been for weeks. Along the canyon road the cows and their calves are back, at least those that have been kept alive the past few months down along the edge of the Pecos. The sound of mothering moos is comforting.

This afternoon's storm was so heavy, I went out to check if the Begoso was flowing. But there was nothing but rain-wet sand. It will take many such storms to saturate this thirsty earth to excess. The coyotes, as they do after every storm, were hollering like a schoolyard at recess. I could well understand their joy; at last there were puddles to drink from cupped in the stone-hard dirt pockets of the meadows.

Beside the fence gate is a huge pile of firewood, payment last February for a second month of last year's leftover grass for my neighbor Andrés's cows—cows that since were shipped off to Belen. The storm has left the grass around the cabin safe from fire. I fish deep into the woodpile for some dry pieces and build my first fire in weeks. Dinner will be steak and sweet corn grilled on the firepit.

Anu and I celebrate the fire late into the evening, he working on the bones and cobs while I watch the lightning stabbing the night miles away over the eastern prairie.

10

Andelecio had warned me that there might be snakes lurking in the storeroom on that day last summer when I first saw the cabin. If there were, I didn't know it. Just the possibility kept me from doing anything other than fearfully poking my nose in the door. A year has passed since then. The population of rats that had constructed a civilization of weedy nests has long been cleaned out. And kept out with the help of boxes of d-CON that I set out under the storeroom shelves, pushed beyond the reach of Anu's curious nose. I set these boxes out whenever I leave. I put them under the pie chest in the kitchen as well, and under the chest of drawers in the bedroom. And the d-CON has worked well. As for the storeroom, I'm less concerned about the rats themselves—they can easily run in and out of there through the hole in the door Natividad cut for his cats—I just don't want them in there; I don't want any invitations to dinner for a snake.

I brought out a cat to live in the storeroom. I thought a cat would take care of the rat problem better than d-CON. Some cats even develop a knack for doing in rattlesnakes, and I hoped maybe this cat would learn to deal with any of these that might come slithering around. The cat was a female, a stray that a friend had found up in the Santa Fe Canyon. She was headed for the pound, but I took her to the cabin instead. The cat lasted only a couple of weeks, but her demise was not the result of being preyed upon by any Begoso critters. I had brought out my neighbor's dog from Santa Fe to play with Anu for the week we would be staying at the cabin. My neighbor's dog saw the cat the moment I let him out of the truck. Chased her, caught her, killed her. I was so mad at the dog, I considered promptly putting him back in the truck, driving him back to Santa Fe, and dumping him in my neighbor's yard. But I calmed down for Anu's sake and let him stay. I took the dead cat and climbed up to the top of a juniper tree and put her body on the highest branch for the benefit of some passing owl.

I tried another cat a few weeks later. This one was fierce. He was making a nuisance of himself attacking all the other cats in my Santa Fe neighborhood. He was on his way to the pound too. I thought he would be just the thing for my storeroom. He hung around the cabin for most of a day and then took off. I haven't seen him since. So now I'm back to pushing boxes of d-CON under things. And worrying about snakes.

One day when Seferino stopped by for a visit on his way to his south pasture, he told me about the six-foot rattler skin that Natividad had kept tacked up on the cabin wall.

"Caught that snake right here on the *portal* one night," Seferino said. "Skinned him and ate him."

"But that was a long time ago," I said. "I haven't seen any snakes around here now."

"Well, I hope you don't," he said, "but be careful just the same.

Ran into one just last week up on the mesa. Blackie saw it first and barked."

"What did you do?" I asked.

"Killed it with the shovel I keep in the back of my truck."

☙

rat·tle·snake . . . *n* (1630): any of the American pit vipers comprising two genera (Crotalus and Sistrurus) and having horny interlocking joints at the end of the tail that make a sharp rattling sound when shaken (Merriam Webster's Collegiate Dictionary, Tenth Edition)

Is this all you have to say, Mr. Webster? You do not mention that these pit vipers range in length from one to six or more feet. That they have bands circling their bodies that can be yellow and green or black and gray or just about any color in between. You do not mention that these pit vipers especially like to hang out in woodpiles and storerooms, under rocks or in meadow grass or under chamisa bushes. You do not mention that they are utterly terrifying to some humans, causing a severe case of *tremens* merely at the sight of one. Nor do you mention that these terrified humans can have fitful nights filled with evil snake dreams for weeks after having observed one slowly slithering around the doors of a cabin.

I am one of those people who is utterly, irrationally, and hopelessly terrified of snakes. My politically correct ecological consciousness breaks down completely at the sight of a snake. Friends tell me: Don't worry, snakes are bound to be more frightened of you than you are of them. I doubt that. Nothing could be as scared of me as I am of snakes. I remember once taking a psychology class in college where the class was shown a film in which a scientist put a de-venomed snake in a crib with a baby to prove that babies are not instinctively afraid of snakes. The scientist made his point, but I could barely sit still to watch the infant crawl up to play with the new toy in the crib. I was not convinced. Maybe this instinct doesn't develop till later.

I don't recall ever meeting a snake until I was maybe ten years old. I grew up in the city, and there weren't any snakes around to meet. So that one was my first snake. It was lying across a hiking trail in the mountains, and when I saw it I froze in horror. Now, isn't that instinct? I don't even know if it was poisonous. It was a snake; that was enough.

And don't tell me humankind hasn't made the snake into the symbol of ultimate evil, starting for us Westerners in the Garden of Eden. Ever since, all manifestation of things horrifying has taken on the image of the snake. There were Laocoön and his kids with those writhing serpents, Cleopatra with her asp, and that ghastly hairdo of Medusa. In the Norse myth of the end of the universe, who but Midgard the Serpent will bring it all crashing down? And before Midgard gets the chance to finish us off, Indra has to decapitate Vitra, the serpent of chaos, just to get things started. Dragons sometimes have feet, sometimes not, but they all tend to undulate a lot. And sea monsters are definitely serpentine. Even among the Pecos Indians, who once hunted down their dinner in Begoso Canyon, there is a legend about a giant hissing serpent that took up residence at the bottom of their kiva. They had a heck of a time getting it out of there. But when they finally roped it, hauled it up, and dumped it into the river, rain began to fall. The long drought was at an end. Scientists can experiment with babies all they want. All of mythic history tells us that snakes are evil. No scientist can convince me otherwise.

I have now met the Snake from Hell. It was on a lovely fall Begoso morning. My son Tonio, who was on vacation visiting me for a few days, was sitting on the bench under the *portal* reading his favorite book of the moment: *Windows '95*. I was in the bedroom sweeping the rug.

Suddenly Tonio called out "rattlesnake!" And a split second later: "BIG RATTLESNAKE!"

I rushed out of the cabin to look. The biggest, ugliest, most terrifying monster I have ever seen was slowly winding its way into the yard through the open fence gate. It was easily six feet long— no, I'm NOT exaggerating—and its body, decorated with bilious green and yellow bands, speckled all over with black dots, was thick as a man's fist. My first thought was, Where's Anu? Tonio spied him outside the fence, lying in the shade of the truck. He hadn't yet seen the snake. Tonio sprang over the five-foot wire hog fence, grabbed Anu, and shut him into the truck cab. Then he climbed back over the fence and stood with me at a safe distance out in the yard.

Meanwhile the venomous viper had arrived at the storeroom door, which was standing wide open. Slowly it slithered its long body through the doorway. When it was all the way inside, I ran quickly back to the cabin, shut tight the doors to the bedroom and kitchen, and ran back into the yard. Tonio and I stood with our eyes glued to the storeroom door. Certainly we had both encountered rattlesnakes before, but these had been of a reasonable size for a snake. Although I was afraid of them, they did indeed seem as eager to avoid me as I was to avoid them. But neither of us had ever seen a monster like this! My heart was pounding like the boom box on a low-rider: Tonio wasn't exactly calm either.

"What if it doesn't come out of there?" I asked, not really expecting an answer. I had visions of waiting around for hours at the pleasure of this serpent, while it did whatever it was planning to do in the storeroom. A good ten minutes went by while Tonio and I discussed the little we knew of the characteristics of snakes.

"I'm told they can only strike half their distance," Tonio said.

"Great, but that means one of us would have to get within four feet of that thing to swing the shovel at it. And besides, the shovel's in the storeroom with the snake."

"Well, we could throw a rock at it," Tonio suggested.

"That snake is so fat," I countered, "a rock would probably just make it mad, and it might come after us."

After a while, the viper poked its ugly nose out of the storeroom. It waved its head back and forth, as if to decide which direction it would take, and then slowly slithered up onto the *portal*. The snake wound itself over to the closed bedroom door, raised the top of its body up like a cobra rising from a basket, and swayed with an eerie, evil grace around the edges of the door, searching for a way in. Apparently disappointed at finding no entry, it slowly moved on toward the kitchen door and raised itself up again. I wondered if it had been here before; it certainly seemed to know where the doors are. And perhaps it might know that those panels it was checking out are sometimes open. After several passes across the door with its huge head, it gave up on the kitchen as well and undulated slowly over to the woodpile stacked on the *portal* just to the left of the door.

"There may be rats down in the wood," I said. I have often seen rat droppings around the woodpile, and sometimes I've had to pick up a stiff, d-CON-dead rat and dump it into a plastic bag to put in the garbage. The reptile moved up the pile, winding itself up to the top. It would climb by looping the head end of its body onto a piece of stove wood, then bringing up its center, then bringing up its tail. It moved with deliberation, writhing slowly through the stack, poking its head into spaces between the logs. Apparently my d-CON treatments of the woodpile were successful; the monster didn't find anything that interested it. But it took its own sweet time looking. Then slowly it descended to the floor of the *portal* in a reverse of the looping manner it had used to get up. It turned the corner of the cabin and undulated slowly around through the bushes along the front stone wall, finally exiting through the open fence gate that leads to the outhouse and Natividad's old sheep corral.

"God, I hope it doesn't head for the outhouse!" I said to Tonio. I had fearsome thoughts of it taking up residence in there.

"Yes, that would be exceedingly inconvenient," Tonio laughed. But the snake didn't take the turn to the outhouse. It moved on into the meadow in the direction of the sheep corral. At this point Tonio, overcome by a burst of courage, picked up a huge rock and went after the snake. He threw the rock, but it was so heavy it fell short. He did manage to infuriate the monster, however, which coiled and set off its rattles with a sound like an electric buzzer gone haywire. Tonio jumped back out of its range. Finding nothing to strike, the viper uncoiled and continued on its way into the meadow and out of sight.

Well, at least it was gone. The snake had taken a good half hour to check out the place. I had no desire to stay at the cabin a moment longer. The serpent had violated my Garden of Eden, and I just wanted to get away from there. Tonio and I quickly gathered up our things and tossed them into the truck, locked up the cabin, and left. Anu had missed the whole performance. He was curled up asleep on the cab seat.

We needed to stop for gas at the Pueblo Bar. My hand was still shaking when I put the nozzle into the gas tank. I went in to pay Elizardo. Of course I had to tell him about the snake.

"I'm not stretching the size," I said. "It really was six feet long."

"Oh, I believe you," Elizardo said. "I've seen 'em longer than that around here. In fact, one day when I was out at my ranch. . . ." I was in no mood for snake stories.

"Well, why didn't you shoot it?" Elizardo asked. I confessed, rather sheepishly, that I didn't own a gun.

"You mean you don't have a gun out there?" Elizardo asked in amazement. I felt embarrassed that I was such an inadequate Begoso canyoneer.

"But," I said, "I'm going to get one. Today if I can." The bar's clientele were highly amused at the whole exchange.

I went out to the truck and told Tonio we were going to stop and buy a gun on the way back into Santa Fe.

"A gun?" Tonio, my city-bred son, said. "I don't like guns; they're dangerous."

"I don't like them either, but if that viper ever comes back I'm going to blast him. I won't stay out there in that canyon without a gun from now on."

"Okay, Mom," he laughed; "let's go buy your gun. Next thing we know, you'll be joining the NRA!"

We stopped at the Walmart on Cerrillos Road. I picked out a twelve-gauge shotgun in the sporting goods section. I wanted something that would scatter shot in the general direction of what I was pointing at. I knew I'd never hit that snake with a single bullet, especially if my hands were shaking.

The gun was certainly no Uzi, but still I had to sign a federal form to buy it. The form asked what the gun would be used for. Of the list of things one was supposed to check off—hunting, target practice, competitions, etc.—there was no mention of snakes. The closest item was "self-protection." I doubted protection from snakes was what this item meant, but I checked it anyway. I'll probably go down in government statistics as another woman buying a gun to shoot intruders. The manager of the store said I couldn't buy the shotgun shells at the same time I bought the gun. Another federal regulation. In case I might decide to shoot up the place on my way out, I suppose. But then he obligingly offered to carry the gun out to the truck for me, where I could leave it, and then I could come back in and buy the shot.

When we got home, I phoned a friend who is a hunter and told him I wanted him to teach me to shoot. I spent several hours with him shooting at beer cans on his property near Santa Fe. At first I missed them all. But after a while they began to show holes, so at least some of the shot was getting close enough. Close enough was all I cared about.

Tonio went back to work in San Francisco, leaving me to my target practice. The serpent writhed through my dreams in all its mythic evil for several nights running, but days I was angry with myself. I'm not going to let that snake ruin my life!

Of course I babbled on and on to my friends about the viper's visitation. In the main, they were not in the least sympathetic. They disapproved of my vows to murder the beast, offering suggestions on how I might catch it in some sort of container and release it somewhere far away. They just didn't get it. My ecological concerns do not extend to rattlesnakes. The snake elicited in me a sense of terror that has nothing to do with reason. I did not simply want to "remove" it, even if I could have figured out a way to do so safely. So long as that snake was alive, my desire to kill it was equally as mythic as my fear of it.

A week later I drove out to the cabin with my gun. When I got to the cabin gate, I sat in the cab and loaded the shells. Then I shut Anu in the cab, took the loaded gun, and stalked the property. I checked out the storeroom, threw pieces of wood at the woodpile, prowled through the yard inside the fence, and cautiously opened the door to the outhouse. No snake. Then I advanced on the sheep corral, stepping carefully through the tall grass. I threw rocks at the stone walls to see if I could elicit a response. If the viper was there, it didn't show itself. I was both relieved and disappointed. I carefully picked my way back to the cabin, set the safety on the gun, and leaned it up against the cabin wall. I let Anu out of the truck, and after he was in the yard, I closed the gates to keep him in.

Anu immediately went over to the front gate and tried to paw it open. Although I was worried about the snake, I realized I couldn't keep the poor dog cooped up in the yard all week. I finally decided I had to let him out, and he ran off joyously into the meadow. I unloaded the groceries from the truck and took them into the kitchen. But every few minutes I would go out and check to see what Anu was about.

It took me a few days to calm down. With my new shotgun at the ready I felt safe enough. As for Anu's safety, there is really nothing much I can do. He needs to be free to roam. If the snake bites him, at least I have the address of the emergency vet thirty miles away in Las Vegas.

Over the next few days, I began to realize that the presence of that huge snake lurking somewhere out in the meadow, or maybe just behind the cabin, or perhaps up by the outhouse, or maybe sunning itself on any number of rocky outcrops that are everywhere in the canyon was not just frightening, it was exciting. It gave an edge to my sense of solitude, a heightened awareness of the incipient

danger in the nature around me that I had previously refused to acknowledge. A balance had been added to my somewhat sentimen-
tal embrace of the rugged beauty of the canyon.

A month later the monster was back. This time it was under
the wisteria vine I had planted in the corner of the yard, just inside
the fence. I had finished washing the dinner dishes and was carrying the dishwater out to water the vine. Just as I leaned over to pour
it, the fearsome buzzer went off right at my feet. The same fat bilious green and yellow body was coiled under the leaves. I dropped
the dishpan of water on the snake and ran back to the cabin, grabbed
Anu, who was sitting by the firepit, and dragged him inside by his
collar. I slammed the door and got out the gun. By now I was no
longer keeping it loaded. I rummaged through the drawer where I
keep the shot, loaded up, and keeping Anu shut in behind me, cautiously advanced out into the yard, the gun pointed straight ahead.
But when I got near the vine, I could see the viper was gone. I
looked all around the yard, but it wasn't there. It must have gone
through the fence into the meadow, since it wouldn't have had time
to get to the gate. The crosspieces of hog wire are wide apart. I realized this means that it can come into the yard any time it pleases,
even when the gates are shut.

It was getting dark, so I didn't pursue the beast out in the
meadow. But the next morning I got up at dawn, put on my boots,
and still in my nightgown, took the gun and prowled all around the
outside of the cabin, the edges of the hog fence, up to the outhouse
and sheep corral, and out along the meadow road. Anyone observ-
ing me stalking around the meadow in my boots and pink-and-
white flowered nightgown would have thought he was seeing a vision of Annie Oakley come back to haunt Begoso Canyon. But of
course there's no one around for miles.

I couldn't find it. The snake could have been hiding under the broad leaves of the calabasilla vines just beyond the fence or up on the ridge a mile away by now. With my shotgun gripped tight, pointed straight out in front of me, I was no longer scared. I was mad. I was on a rampage. I was out to kill.

Of course, whenever I stop now to buy gas at the Pueblo Bar, Elizardo always asks me with a grin, "Seen any snakes lately?"

"No, but I'm going to get that snake," I answer. "He's still out there somewhere, and I'm going to kill him!"

"Well, he'll be going to sleep for the winter soon, it's already September." This is certainly a relief. I can spend the winter in peace, knowing I won't have to keep a loaded gun propped against the wall of the bedroom. And Anu can play all day in the snowy meadow if he likes, without my worrying what he's up to. At least not until next March, when the sun warms the earth again, and snakes come winding up out of their holes, voraciously hungry after a long winter's sleep.

11

The purple Michaelmas asters growing along the banks of Begoso Creek are in full bloom today, for this is the feast day of Saint Michael the Archangel. I got up very early this morning so as not to miss the fiesta parade. I fed Anu his breakfast, and then the two of us took off down the dirt road, Anu chasing behind the truck, stopping to rest at the cattle gates. When we got to the paved highway at the Pueblo gate, Anu jumped into the cab with me and we drove the five miles up to the old church at San Miguel.

For several weeks now, the parishioners have been preparing for the celebration of their patron saint. The fiesta committees have organized concessions and raffles, food booths and dance music. The mission villagers have decorated the beds of their pickup truck floats with puffs of paper flowers and banners. The mayordomo has seen to it that the old church has been thoroughly cleaned, and the big bell, mounted on a low frame in the forecourt outside the church door, given a fresh coat of shiny gold paint. The parish bulletin promises that for five dollars a fling, the priest will dance with you. All for the greater glory of the archangel and the church restoration fund.

The parade was in full swing when I arrived at the crowded plaza in front of the church. I found a place to park at the back of the church parking lot, left Anu shut in the cab, and went off to see the show: people on horseback, in cars, on motorcycles, or just walking along the half-mile parade route from the Ribera post office to San Miguel. The signs on the side panels of the pickup floats announced their village churches: Our Lady of Guadalupe, San Juan de Nepomocena, San José del Bado, San Isidro Labrador, Santa Rita de Casia, Nuestra Señora del Rosario, San Antonio de Padua. Inside the bowers of crepe paper on the truck beds, the tasseled silk church banners were held high by the riders. On arrival at the plaza, the riders jumped off and carried their banners into the church, while the pickup drivers drove off to find a place to park.

In the parish hall women were selling handmade knitted pot holders, crocheted doilies, embroidered dish towels and pillow covers, as well as white elephant knickknacks that people had donated for the sale. One could buy fresh-baked pies and cakes and breads, hot dogs and hamburgers smothered in green chile and wrapped in tortillas. The delicious smell of carnitas and chicharones frying in huge pots mingled with the aroma of bread baking in the beehive-shaped community *horno,* the adobe bread oven on the plaza. I bought some carnitas from Mike, the self-proclaimed Carnitas King of the Valley, for a late breakfast. And at the bakery booth, a pineapple pie to take back to the cabin from a lady I'd met at the post office.

Down by the river a band was playing, and couples were dancing on a cement platform in the warm morning sun. The priest hadn't yet arrived to offer his five-dollars-a-dance services. There was a dart-throw booth, where the children bought three tries to pop a balloon, and a ring toss, where they tried to throttle a plastic duck floating around in a wading pool. In the little school building next to the church was a cakewalk: the winner won one of the many donated big goo-frosted cakes if he or she were standing on the right number pasted on the floor when the music stopped. One booth was selling T-shirts in all sorts of colors, each sporting a picture of San Miguel church on the front.

"I'll take a green one," I said to the man in the booth, and went back to my truck to put it on for the celebration. Poor Anu was hanging his head out the truck window looking extremely sad, longing to join the fun. Labradors are people dogs and always want to be where the action is. I pacified him for the moment with the remainder of my breakfast carnitas.

When I got back to the plaza wearing my new T-shirt, I encountered Jesus. He was strolling through the plaza, a thin, long-haired and bearded young man who had just stepped out through the frame of a Renaissance painting. He was wearing one of the priest's white robes, with a red bedspread draped jauntily over one shoulder. Jesus offered me his blessing, then moved on to bestow blessings on every side as he passed through the crowd. Just before eleven, the newly goldened church bell rang. The Mass for San Miguel Arcangel was about to start.

San Miguel church was completed by the land grant settlers in 1806. It was built as a fortress, with walls three feet thick and twenty feet high to protect the villagers from Indian attacks. There are two bell towers on either side of the entrance. Originally these towers were higher than they are today and served as watchtowers. When the settlers sighted a band of Indians riding toward the village, they rang the church bells and people ran for cover inside. As I walked up the steps to the forecourt of the old church, I stopped for a moment to look at the huge crucifix that stands at the top of the steps. Jesus came up behind me.

"My father, my earthly one, that is," he corrected himself with a grin, "made that for the church." The figure of Christ is made from railroad spikes, the head surrounded by a halo made from a rusted clutch wheel. The sculpture is so cleverly contrived that I had to look closely to see how it was made.

Inside, the church was packed. People were sitting up in the loft and standing along the walls. In one of the back pews two little girls squeezed together to make room for me to sit. The banners from the mission churches were displayed across the front of the church. Resting on a table at the bottom of the steps to the altar was a small, ornate plaster statue of San Miguel, one foot stomping on a dragon-devil, with handles coming out from the base of the statue so he could be carried.

The huge bell outside rang again, and a small band of guitars at the front of the church struck up the entrance processional. We all stood as the procession started down the aisle: the lectors and altar boys, an old man carrying a rough wooden cross, two men carrying the banner of the Las Vegas chapter of the Knights of Columbus, and Jesus in his robe and bedspread. The priest came last, wearing a gold-threaded white chasuble, embroidered on the front with a picture of Saint Michael slaying the devil with a huge pitchfork. When the procession reached the front of the church, the priest stepped up to the podium, gave us his blessing, and recited the special prayer to Saint Michael, petitioning the archangel "to thrust into hell Satan and all the other evil spirits who roam through the world seeking the ruin of souls."

The Mass continued with the readings from the Scriptures. I looked around the church. Lavish bouquets of flowers, donated by the parishioners, were set out all about the transept and the altar, surrounded with flickering candles. The banners from the village churches that flanked the nave gave a bright festive air to the celebration. I thought of how much this old church had changed over its long history. The large gothic-shaped windows, which filtered the late-morning sunlight into our celebration, were once only narrow slits along the thick side walls. Through these slits the besieged settlers could shoot at the attacking Indians. The wooden floor now supports rows of hand-carved pews; we are all sitting on the bones of the early worshipers buried below. The original floor of the church was dirt, marked off in rectangles to provide safe accommodation for the settlers in their final rest—safe in that the graves wouldn't be dug up to get the burial blankets or scalps of the recently departed souls.

In my readings of the history of the land grant, I came across some accounts of the religious rites in this church in the journals of the Santa Fe Trail traders. One of these I found in the journal of Matt Field, a reporter from the *New Orleans Picayune*. Field made the trek across the plains to New Mexico in 1839. His caravan had stopped for the night in San Miguel, and he recorded his impressions of the church:

Finding that the Spanish caravan did not intend to start until the next day, full time was allowed to witness the religious ceremonies in the church. . . . There were no seats of any kind in the church, and the worshippers were all either standing or kneeling. The mud walls were whitewashed, and a few wretched daubs of paintings, actually frightful to look at, were fastened up, some to rude frames, others hanging in rags with no frame at all. . . . In a recess at one side of the altar, stood two men, one playing a fiddle and the other a guitar, and on those instruments the musicians seemed to be studying what kind of an extravagant and fantastic discord they could make. The noise made by two quarrelsome cats was quite as much like music. . . . In a few moments a priest appeared from an apartment at one side of the altar, and with great precipitation commenced his duties. He kicked open a door in the wooden railing of the altar and advanced among the people . . . and dipping his brush in the sacred fluid, he sprinkled the congregation, flirting his brush about and muttering blessings, much more like an angry housewife, scurrying about and scolding servants, than a man of God. . . . [T]hough pure religion may have existed in that motley congregation, it was an offensive libel on sacred things. . . . Fifteen minutes after, the

writer found [the priest] smoking a chupar in the shop of
the only American trader in town.[22]

Since the date is 1839, the only American in town must have been Thomas Rowland, who would some years later meet a mysterious and grisly end.

It was difficult to believe that the dignified and formal ritual that was being recited in front of me was once carried out here by a priest muttering like an angry housewife, assuredly in those times a Latin-speaking housewife.

The plaster-cast statues of the Virgin and Jesus at each side of the transept, the San Miguel in his niche high on the apse wall, the saints in the window openings, and the two, near-human-size angels that bow toward each other at the altar are gifts to the church from the clergy and members of the congregation over the years. But so were the hand-carved folk pieces that these statues replaced, folk pieces that were casually tossed out by the parish priest, Father Fayet, in the nineteenth century.

Father Fayet was a Frenchman, brought to New Mexico by Bishop Lamy in 1856 to help the bishop clean up the clerical corruption that had festered in the territory during the period of Mexican control. And while Lamy and his imported priests are well remembered in New Mexico for their clerical reforms and their attempts to combat the appalling illiteracy through the establishment of parochial schools (in the 1880s Father Fayet built a school for San Miguel at his own expense), they are also remembered with bitterness for their contemptuous dismissal and destruction of many of the carvings and paintings of religious figures that were the artistic impulses of a people's faith.

Father Fayet presided over San Miguel from 1866 to 1900. He

not only held strong views on the inappropriateness of what his parishioners had considered ecclesiastic art, he also set about to redo the architecture of San Miguel church "in good taste," to use his own words.²³ He redesigned the bell towers; replaced the old flat roof with a pitched one, covering up the four-foot-high ramparts from the church's days as a fortress; and enlarged the windows in the gothic style. Inside, he hid the old vigas with a dropped clapboard ceiling and constructed a trellis-covered arch in front of the apse. Father Fayet did much of the work himself to bring his artistic concepts to architectural fruition. He had a sense of the flamboyant and the splendorous, and is said to have thrown some spectacular processions. He loved fiestas, and could be found at most all of them in San Miguel County and beyond.

But the Reverend Jean B. Fayet was not a man to be fooled with. He was huge, brawny, and given to bursts of temper. There is a story of Father Fayet throwing a workman off the church tower because of an insulting remark. The man survived his crash landing, ran into the woods, and wouldn't come out for a week for fear of the priest. And another about a thief who attempted to hold up the good priest and rob the church strongbox. Father Fayet easily disarmed the man, picked him up, and set him, bottom down, on top a burning woodstove. In 1879 — so it is said — the priest took on saintly, even miraculous dimensions when, during a grasshopper infestation that was ruining the crops, he walked out into the fields sprinkling holy water in all directions. Within twenty-four hours the grasshoppers had fled. In the plaster props that people the wall niches and altar, in the dropped ceiling and proscenium arch, Father Fayet's architectural legacy of "good taste" still lives on as the stage set for the celebration enacted in the old church this morning.²⁴

When the bread and wine had been distributed to the congregation, the priest announced that the procession of the patron saint would now begin. The band of guitars led the way down the aisle from the altar, playing and singing an old Spanish hymn to the Virgin: "Con el angel de María las grandezas celebrad; transportados de alegría sus finezas publicad." They walked out into the warm noon sunshine, followed by parishioners carrying the many mission church banners. Then the statue of San Miguel, waiting at the foot of the altar, was picked up by four men and carried down the aisle and out the door. We all filed out of the church behind the statue, Jesus and the priest bringing up the rear.

As I walked along in the procession behind the statue, I was again reminded of a description I had read of such a procession for the village saint. This one was written by George Kendall, the reporter from Louisiana who was incarcerated in San Miguel. He describes the procession as he watched it from the window of his jail cell on the plaza a hundred fifty years ago:

> *A more comical figure than this same San Miguel it would be difficult to either imagine or discover. I cannot say his saintship had ever been tarred, but he had certainly been feathered from head to foot. From his shoulders hung list-lessly a pair of huge, ill-constructed wings; his face that of a large doll, while his head, to complete this ludicrous tout ensemble, was covered with a lace cap of the fashion of our grandmothers. First came an old, bald-headed priest, a coarse, dirty blanket tied about him with a piece of rope, an open prayer book in his hand, a rude wooden cross hanging*

from his neck, and a pair of spectacles on his nose . . . about the size of common teacups, and set in wide rims of buffalo horn. Following close at the heels of this odd figure came our particular friend, Juan Sandobal, strumming his crazy mandolin, and digging from it the only tune within his musical scope. By his side walked a brother artist, zealously sawing away on a rusty violin. . . . As each of these performers knew but one tune, and as both were playing at the same time, the reader . . . can easily imagine the effect. . . . Nothing could be more grotesque and laughable than this comical head of St. Michael, enveloped in an old-fashioned lady's cap, rising and falling with every motion of the car on which it was borne.[25]

It is ironic that the statue of San Miguel that Kendall is describing with such amused forbearance is most likely the same statue that now resides in the Taylor Museum in Colorado. The museum bought it from a Santa Fe collector in 1938 for two hundred dollars. It is known that the San Miguel survived Father Fayet's late nineteenth-century purges, but a few years later it was either pilfered from the church by some simoniac or tossed out by yet another clergyman who found such homemade expressions of faith out of fashion. Were the statue to have a price tag today, it would be in the many thousands.[26]

The church at San Miguel is noted for having had a number of eccentric priests in addition to the two mentioned in the Americans' trail journals and the saintly, if intemperate, Father Fayet. The Reverend John Peter Moog, a native of Flanders, followed the French priest to the San Miguel pulpit a few years later. Father Moog was equally as intemperate as his predecessor. He presided over San Miguel for almost forty years, and old-timers still remember his iron-fisted rule. As an extension of his spiritual services to the community, the priest, together with one of his parishioners, provided the village hooch from their private still during Prohibition.

Father Moog was considered by many to be endowed with awesome powers of darkness. In the church archives, I came across a 1928 letter from Archbishop Gerken of Santa Fe to the parish of San Miguel in which His Eminence offers his condolences to the parishioners for the unfortunate happenstance that Father Moog was socked in the face by an irate member of his flock. In dealing with this affront, Father Moog did not heed the advice of his spiritual master and turn the other cheek. Rumor has it that he laid a curse upon the perpetrator of this dastardly deed and upon all his children.

The most notorious of all the San Miguel shepherds, however, was Father José Francisco Leyba y Rosas, the patriot priest involved in the uprising against the American takeover. Father Leyba reigned over San Miguel off and on from 1829 until he was buried under the church floor in 1856. In addition to his revolutionary political tendencies, he was a gambler, a drunkard, and a philanderer. He borrowed, but neglected to return, the money from the bishop's Poor Souls Fund. Because of his debts, it seems someone was always suing him. He did indeed start a school in San Miguel—in the 1830s one of only three schools in New Mexico. However, one can only wonder what kind of an education the children received from the lecherous clergyman. Father Leyba loved to booze it up with the trail traders and even—despite his earlier revolutionary leanings—with the American officers. After one of his bouts with them, an officer writes: "On leaving camp, [Leyba] mounted his pony and rode around the camp at the fastest run of his horse . . . raising his hat with a grand flourish [and] gave us the parting 'Adios! Goodbye! Go to Hell!'"[27]

The correct and proper Frenchman Bishop Lamy was appalled at Leyba's behavior. Soon after his arrival in New Mexico, the bishop had had to temporarily relieve the clergyman of his post, since Leyba was unable to carry out his priestly duties. He had fallen off his horse drunk and broken his leg in three places. But Lamy couldn't afford to get rid of the profligate priest altogether, since at that time Leyba was one of only a very few New Mexican priests in the entire territory.

Despite the antics of the village priests and the seemingly strange rituals and habits of the people, there is more behind the words of the trail journalists and other nineteenth-century American writers' responses to the New Mexican villagers' religious ceremonies than just patronizing descriptions of amusing encounters with another culture, or as condemnations of them as "an offensive libel on sacred things." Perhaps the point is that the Spanish love of images and pageantry in itself is foreign to the Anglo sense of religious decorum, whether Protestant *or* Catholic. I am again reminded of my years in Spain. There, for centuries, the religious processions have been carried out with a pomp fit for the majesty of royalty. But then in Spain, Christ *is* king, and both he and his mother, as well as his brother and sister saints are dressed in the finest jewel-embroidered velvet, crowned in gold, and carried through the streets during holy days on ornate palanquins of sculpted silver. The rude interior of the San Miguel church and the "ludicrous" Saint Michael with the bobbing head that these accounts describe are the humble efforts of a culture to spiritually transcend the ruthless poverty of

a frontier world. People make do with what they have, be it only feathers and someone's grandmother's lace cap. And yet the religious flamboyance of Spain, of which these nineteenth-century village rituals are the relic of a half-forgotten idea, is even today distasteful to many people, let alone symbolic of the excesses that verge on an almost pagan worship of idols—a worship that the soldiers of the Reformation were unable to curb.

Our simple and solemn procession around the San Miguel church today was as little like the one Kendall described as was the ceremony in the church itself like that described by Matt Field. Nor did it have any of the pomp of Spain. Still, these ritual events of Saint Michael's fiesta this warm September morning are the echoes of a collective cultural memory, not just of Hispanic life on the frontier of a New World but also of the Old World traditions that crossed the ocean with the settlers centuries ago.

Our procession moved out to the graveyard behind the church and finally came back around to the front entrance again. We returned to our places in the pews for the priest to give us his final blessing and formally end the Mass. And then, confident that Saint Michael now had well in hand all those evil spirits that roam through the world seeking the ruin of souls, we headed back out to the fiesta to eat hot dogs and chicharones and to dance with the priest.

Epilogue

Two years of seasons have passed since I first rounded the rise in the meadow and discovered Natividad's cabin in the distance. Autumn has come round again, and the leaves of the young cottonwoods at the edge of Begoso Creek are working their way from green to gold. My friend Anu is no longer a puppy. His paws are tough now from the miles he has traveled, and he heralds our visitors with a deep-throated, full-grown bark. The summer drought this year ended in a flood of storms, and the water in Natividad's well is now far above the silt line. I no longer need to haul gas cans of water out from town. And the soothsayers at the weather bureau predict a heavy snowpack this winter.

Last winter's cold taught me that I needed to make a change to Natividad's cabin: a third woodstove. This one in the small eating room off the kitchen so I won't have to dress for dinner huddled in my goose-down parka. I found a narrow potbelly in a garage sale and hired one of the villagers to come out and poke the stovepipe through the stone ceiling and up through the tin roof.

The drought changed my plans for making chokecherry wine; the hedge is now just dry sticks in the ground. The rains came too late to save one of the apple trees I put in last spring, and the vines that I planted with such expectation along Anu's hog fence are crisp brown skeletons splayed against the wire. Natividad's plum orchard, however, is doing fine—it has survived worse droughts than this one. And with the late summer rains, the meadows are green and lush. The yellow and purple flowers of September are back again, and the feathery tips of the grama grass smartly salute each other in the wind.

A few weeks ago the snake-monster returned. I found him stretched out full length, sunning himself next to the warm stones of the wall at the back of the cabin. Despite my sudden panic, it was not without shame that I took my shotgun and killed him. At my first encounter with him, I was in a rage that he had invaded my peaceful canyon world. But as I took the shovel and picked up his mangled body full of buckshot and hung it on a tree branch some distance from the cabin, I realized that it was not he who had invaded my world but I who had invaded his. Rattlesnakes are territorial. For years he must have had full run of the place. Perhaps not since Natividad died some thirty years ago, abandoning the cabin to the rats and rabbits and lizards, had anyone challenged his turf. And then I had arrived, rumbling down the canyon in my Toyota, building fences, poisoning his dinner rats, bringing a dog to chase his rabbits, practicing for his murder shooting beer cans in the meadow. Of course the snake had to die. There was no room in his territory for the both of us. At least for a while, Anu and I are safe. And if or when another of his kind realizes the grand old viper has vacated his claim and the territory is again up for grabs, I'll kill him too. Yet, the killing humbled me. Perhaps the snake had to be dead before I could consider its life with any small amount of equanimity. At least I supplied a hawk or an owl or some other Begoso critter with a quick and easy meal, for when I went back to check the tree branch half an hour later, the riddled body was gone.

Down in San Miguel, the saint's fiesta has come and gone, and there won't be another feast like that one until the villagers vie with each other to see who can throw the most lavish posada this coming Christmas. I won't be stopping by Andelecio's house any more for coffee on Sunday mornings and visiting with his neighbors who drop in after Mass. His house in Ribera is sold, and he has moved to Albuquerque, severing his ties to the valley. Seferino's Fito, the baby bull, has been traded for one of a different bloodline, and Blackie, his dog, is no longer with us.

The villages and the land itself of the old San Miguel del Bado grant have gone through many transitions over the past two hundred years. It was the opening of the Santa Fe Trail that suddenly transformed the isolated villages on the *merced* into an important territorial trading area, exposing a rural folk to people and goods and ideas from another culture. During this time the population of the village of San Miguel grew from 738, according to a parish count, to 2,200, according to the U.S. Territorial Census of 1850. This made San Miguel one of the largest settlements in New Mexican territory. And counting all the villages on the land grant, there were some 4,200 people living in the area. But the development of the town of Las Vegas spelled the decline of San Miguel. San Miguel parish, once extending to all the territory east to the New Mexico border and south along the Pecos into Texas, was reduced in 1857 to a handful of villages. And in 1864 the village lost its status as a U.S. county seat to its burgeoning eastern neighbor. With the closing of the trail and the subsequent loss of the common lands, the population dwindled back down to near what it had been early in the century. Wage work, when it could be found, allowed people to continue to live on their grant properties, at least part of the time, until after the depression. But with the advent of World War II and the work opportunities available in the cities, the villages declined even further. The adobe structures around the plaza of San Miguel were in decay, and there were abandoned houses throughout the villages. The 1970 census counted only 1,700 people in the enumeration district that approximates the original grant area, and the 1990 census counted about the same.

But changes are again upon us. New Mexico is growing and San Miguel County is growing. Between 1980 and 1990 property values have doubled in the county and taxes along with them. Where once the villagers could sustain themselves with a few cattle or sheep and a vegetable plot, this is no longer the case. And, of course, life expectations have changed. The young boy who once spent much of the year on the open range, armed with his bow and arrows and his *boladora,* has left for school or for work in the cities. New rural estate subdivisions are beginning to break up the ranch lands east of Santa Fe along the freeway to Las Vegas. Ivan, the Ribera postmaster, has moved from the tiny office built as an extension of his house. He now presides over a spanking new red-white-and-blue facility, sized to meet the anticipated future.

Along with this growth, the characteristics of the population will change. Although the 1990 census counts more than 90 percent of the population of the villages down the Pecos, south of the freeway, as being of Hispanic origin, in the last few years more and more Anglos have moved into the area. Hence undoubtedly this percentage will decline in the year 2000 census. Some of these newcomers are building houses on subdivided land; others are moving into the villages and refurbishing the old adobes. Many of these new settlers are writers and artists seeking a retreat in the quiet valley villages and the lush cottonwood-lined meadowlands along the river's edge.

Yet despite these inevitable changes, one should not under-estimate the pull of tradition. Most of my neighbors have spent some part of their lives working away from the area. Some only as far as Las Vegas or Albuquerque, some for the railroad or the mines in the northern states, and some much farther afield. And yet they have returned in their later years to pick up again the life they once led here as young people. And because they are heirs of the land grant, they still have the private land that has been in their families for generations. But we will have to wait to know whether their children and grandchildren will come back to claim this heritage.

Begoso Canyon cannot escape these changes. Driving out the dirt road just the other afternoon, I heard the unmistakable sound of a generator. I pulled the truck off the road and went to investigate. A piece of cow pasture, just beyond where I cut loose the mysterious balloons, has been sold. Two newcomers are building a house. Soon Natividad's cabin will have its first live-in neighbors—neighbors with electricity. The new house is a couple of miles from me, but suddenly the feel of the canyon is different. And there is talk down at the Pueblo Bar of further breaking up the pastures along the canyon road and bringing electricity to the new lots.

I take heart that the Begoso cabin is still far away from this activity. My life here is almost as primitive as it was in the log cabin in the Arctic so many years ago. That experience made it easy for me to settle into this new home: I was an old hand at woodstoves and kerosene lamps and well pulleys. Of course today I can drive my truck into town for food and kerosene and even water if I need it in a summer drought. And I don't have to buy one of my neighbor's cows and stab her to death so she can provide me with a winter of dinners. But just as that Arctic world came to an abrupt end only a few years later, I have the feeling that in these last two years I have been fortunate to experience Begoso Canyon just before it, too, changes forever. The change won't be so sudden and drastic as it was in the far north. But with the breaking up of the pastures and the coming of power lines, an agricultural way of life and the traditions that have measured that life from season to season will inevitably dissolve into the waves of a national uniformity.

When I first sighted the little cabin in the distance at the end of the meadow, it had awakened again my instincts to withdraw from the world and simply live in my hermit dream. I was free to do whatever I wished with my life. I felt a little like a modern-day Hindu sannyasi, who having studied and acquired his vocation, managed his household, raised his family, provided a son for the ancestors (I provided my ancestors with two), leaves it all behind and retreats to the woods, free of worldly debts, to live out his days in contemplation of the meaning of it all. But as these seasons have passed, I find myself more and more engaged in the life around me: helping a neighbor dig rocks out of the road or attending a community meeting or reading the liturgy now and then on a Sunday. I even found myself appointed to a committee to find funds to repair the settlers' old church. Perhaps these small things are a part of that meaning that the sannyasi contemplates. And as I said earlier, we are many different people at once; if we were not, our lives would be dull indeed.

But the hermit in me is still very much alive and well. And in the Begoso cabin I have found the perfect retreat from which I can move out on my own terms to encounter the world. The changes that are moving up the canyon are still at a distance, and I am counting on the beauty of the land around me to last at least as long as I do. I have staked my claim to this wondrous canyon. To the sudden surprise of a snow-covered morning, the orange-pink of the mesa walls, the eerie light of the sunsets, the rainbows that span the ridges. To the pungent smell of piñon branches and the soaked red earth after a rain, the wild crashing of Begoso Creek when the thunder subsides and the coyotes rejoice. These things have now become part of me. It is indeed as José Ortega y Gasset has said: "Tell me the landscape in which you live, and I will tell you who you are."

Notes

Part One

1. Leopold, *A Sand County Almanac*, 188.
2. *United States v. Sandoval et al.*, 167 U.S. 278.198 (1897).
3. The details of this attempted swindle are more complicated than noted here. See Earnshaw et al., "A Study of San Miguel del Vado," and Gompert, "The San Miguel del Bado Land Grant." ("Bado" is used for the name of the grant; "Vado" is the modern spelling, although some authors still use the older spelling.)

Part Two

1. Hubbell, *A Country Year*, 195.
2. Rosenbaum, *Mexicano Resistance in the Southwest*, 104–24.
3. Arellano, "The Never-Ending Land Grant Struggle," 15.
4. *Santa Fe New Mexican*, March 20, 1864. Rowland was murdered in 1858. An article discussing possible suspects was published in the *New Mexican* in 1864.
5. Mocho, *Murder and Justice*, 86–92.
6. *Las Vegas (New Mexico) Daily Optic*, April 10, 1880.
7. Kendall, *Narrative of the Texas–Santa Fe Expedition*, 1:337. Recently the manuscript of a folk play dating from the early 1840s was discovered; the play dramatizes Armijo's victory over the Texans. See Espinosa, *The Folklore of Spain in the American Southwest*, 219.

8. Ibid.

9. Davis, *El Gringo,* 293. See also Kenner, *A History of New Mexican–Plains Indian Relations,* 112.

10. Boyd, "The Plaza of San Miguel del Bado," 7–17.

11. *Las Vegas (New Mexico) Daily Optic,* October 2, 4, 6, 1989.

12. Buss, *La Partera;* see appendix.

13. Meredith M. Marmaduke quoted in Ross, "Two Villages on the Pecos," 40.

14. Lee, "Diary of the Mormon Battalion," (October 1967), 294–96.

15. Ibid.

16. Kendall, *Narrative of the Texas–Santa Fe Expedition,* 1:321; Field, *Matt Field on the Santa Fe Trail,* 254–55.

17. Magoffin, *Down the Santa Fe Trail and into Mexico,* 98.

18. Roybal, "Santa Fe's Wild Days," A-1.

19. See interview with Pablo Lopez in Crespin, "San Miguel del Bado."

20. Mills, "New Mexico: San Miguel County."

21. Ortiz, "Legends of the Upper Pecos Valley."

22. Field, *Matt Field on the Santa Fe Trail,* 253.

23. Fayet to Archbishop Lamy of Santa Fe, August 1882.

24. The account of Father Fayet's physical prowess is found in Crocchiola, "San Miguel del Bado"; the grasshopper miracle is recounted in New Mexico Department of Welfare, Rural County Study, "Villanueva."

25. Kendall, *Narrative of the Texas–Santa Fe Expedition,* 1:337.

26. See San Miguel del Vado church files, Archives of the Archdiocese of Santa Fe. According to Stoller in "Three Church Inventories," the statue was in the collection of Alice Bemis Taylor and acquired by her from the collector J. L. Seligman. Stoller believes the statue is eighteenth century and is the same as the one described in the San Miguel church inventory of 1828.

27. Webb, *Adventures in the Santa Fe Trade.*

Bibliography

Arellano, Anselmo. "The Never-Ending Land Grant Struggle." *La Herencia del Norte* 10 (summer 1996).

Armstrong, R. W. "San Miguel." *New Mexico Magazine* 46, no. 2 (February 1968).

Arroyo-Ortiz, Nelson. "Spanish-American Villages of the Pecos River Valley." Typescript, New Mexico State Records Center, 1975.

Ball, Howard. *Justice Downwind: America's Atomic Testing Program in the 1950s.* New York: Oxford University Press, 1986.

Blackman, Frank W. *Spanish Institutions of the Southwest.* Baltimore: Johns Hopkins University Press, 1891.

Bowden, J. J. "Private Land Claims." *Land and Water Law Review* 8 (1973).

———. "Spanish and Mexican Land Grants." *Land and Water Development Review* 8 (1973).

Boyd, E. "The Plaza of San Miguel del Bado." *El Palacio* 77 (1971).

Bradfute, R. Wells. *The Court of Private Land Claims: The Adjudication of Spanish and Mexican Land Grant Titles, 1891–1904.* Albuquerque: University of New Mexico Press, 1975.

Brown, William E. *The Santa Fe Trail.* National Survey of Historic Sites and Buildings. Washington, D.C.: U.S. Department of the Interior, National Park Service, 1963.

———. *The Santa Fe Trail.* St. Louis: Patrice Press, 1988.

Buss, Fran L. *La Partera.* Ann Arbor: University of Michigan Press, 1980.

Carlson, Alvar. *The Spanish-American Homeland.* Baltimore: Johns Hopkins University Press, 1990.

Chavez, Fray Angelico. *Archives of the Archdiocese of Santa Fe, 1678–1900.* Washington, D.C.: Academy of Franciscan History, 1957.

———. *Très Macho—He Said.* Santa Fe: William Gannon, 1985.

Coan, Charles F. *A History of New Mexico.* New York: American Historical Society, 1925.

Cohea, Carol. "Vandals Ruining Priceless San Miguel." *Albuquerque Journal.* December 9, 1974.

Copeland, Fayette. *Kendall of the Picayune.* Norman: University of Oklahoma Press, 1943.

Cordova, Gilbert Benito, ed. "Bibliography of Unpublished Materials Pertaining to Hispanic Culture in New Mexico WPA Writers' Files." New Mexico State Records Center, 1972.

Cortez, Carlos E. *Spanish and Mexican Land Grants.* New York: Arno, 1974.

———. *The New Mexican Hispano.* New York: Arno, 1974.

Crespin, Reynaldo. "San Miguel del Bado." History Seminar Papers, ed. Lynn Perrigo. Donnelly Library, New Mexico Highlands University, Las Vegas, N.M., 1963.

Crocchiola, Rev. Stanley. "San Miguel del Bado: Famous Home of Fabulous Fr. Fayet." *Santa Fe Register,* April 30, 1948.

Cutler, D. C. "The Legacy of the Treaty of Guadalupe Hidalgo." *NMHR* 53 (1978).

Davis, W. W. H. *El Gringo: New Mexico and Her People.* 1857. Reprint, Lincoln: University of Nebraska Press, 1982.

de Buys, William. *Enchantment and Exploitation: The Life and Hard Times of a New Mexico Mountain Range.* Albuquerque: University of New Mexico Press, 1963.

Defouri, James H. *Historical Sketch of the Catholic Church in New Mexico.* San Francisco: McCormic Brothers, 1887.

DuMars, Charles T., and Malcolm Ebright. "Problems of Spanish and Mexican Land Grants in the Southwest: Their Origin and Extent." *Southwest Review* 1, no. 2 (summer 1981).

Earnshaw, Peggy, et al. "A Study of San Miguel del Vado." Typescript, Colorado College, New Mexico State Records Center, 1973.

Eastman, Clyde, and James R. Gray. *Community Grazing: Practice and Potential in New Mexico.* Albuquerque: University of New Mexico Press, 1987.

Ebright, Malcolm. *Land Grants and Lawsuits in Northern New Mexico.* Albuquerque: University of New Mexico Press, 1994.

———. *Spanish and Mexican Land Grants and the Law.* Albuquerque: Sunflower Press, 1989.

Emory, William Hemsley. *Notes of a Military Reconnaissance.* Albuquerque: University of New Mexico Press, 1951.

Espinosa, Aurelio M. *The Folklore of Spain in the American Southwest.* Ed. J. Manuel Espinosa. Norman: University of Oklahoma Press, 1985.

Fayet, Jean B. Letters. San Miguel del Bado File, 1855–1908, Archives of the Archdiocese of Santa Fe.

Field, Matthew C. *Matt Field on the Santa Fe Trail.* Ed. John Sunder. Norman: University of Oklahoma Press, 1960.

Franzwa, Gregory M. *The Santa Fe Trail Revisited.* St. Louis: Patrice Press, 1989.

Gibson, George R. *Journal of a Soldier under Kearny and Doniphan, 1846–1847.* Vol. 3 in Southwest History Series. Ed. Ralph P. Bieber. Glendale, Calif.: Arthur Clark, 1935.

Glasscock, James T. "The Genizaro Outpost of San Miguel del Bado." Typescript, Colorado College, New Mexico State Records Center, 1973.

Gonner, E. C. K. *Common Lands and Enclosure.* New York: Augustus Kelley, 1969.

Gompert, Kent H. "The San Miguel del Bado Land Grant: Corruption and Bribery in Northern New Mexico." Master's thesis, University of New Mexico, 1986.

Gonzales, Nancie L. *The Spanish-Americans: A Heritage of Pride.* Albuquerque: University of New Mexico Press, 1967.

Gregg, Josiah. *Commerce of the Prairies.* 2 vols. New York: H. G. Langley, 1844.

Griswold del Castillo, Richard. *The Treaty of Guadalupe Hidalgo: A Legacy of Conflict.* Norman: University of Oklahoma Press, 1990.

Hall, Emlen. "San Miguel del Bado and the Loss of the Common Lands." *NMHR* 66 (October 1991).

Hill, William E. *The Santa Fe Trail, Yesterday and Today.* Caldwell, Idaho: Caxton Printers, 1992.

Hubbell, Sue. *A Country Year: Living the Questions.* New York: Random House, 1983.

Inman, Henry. *The Old Santa Fe Trail.* New York: Macmillan, 1898.

Julian, George W. "Land Stealing in New Mexico." *North American Review* 145, no. 368 (1887).

Kendall, George Wilkins. *Narrative of the Texas–Santa Fe Expedition.* 2 vols. New York: Harper Brothers, 1846.

Kenner, Charles L. *A History of New Mexican–Plains Indian Relations.* Norman: University of Oklahoma Press, 1969.

Kessell, John. *Kiva, Cross, and Crown.* Washington, D.C.: National Park Service, 1979.

Knowlton, Clark S., ed. "Spanish and Mexican Land Grants in the Southwest: A Symposium." *Social Science Journal* 13, no. 3 (October 1976).

————. "Land Grant Problems among the State's Spanish Americans." *New Mexico Business* 18, no. 6 (June 1967).

Lamar, Howard R. *The Far Southwest: A Territorial History, 1846–1912.* New Haven, Conn.: Yale University Press, 1966.

Lange, Charles H., and Carroll L. Riley, eds. *The Southwestern Journals of Adolph F. Bandelier, 1880 to 1882.* Albuquerque: University of New Mexico Press, 1966.

Larson, Robert. "The White Caps of New Mexico: A Study of Ethnic Militancy in the Southwest." *Pacific Historical Review* 44 (1975).

Las Vegas (New Mexico) Daily Optic. April 10, 1880; October 2, 4, 6, 1989.

Lee, John D. "Diary of the Mormon Battalion Mission." Ed. Juanita Brooks. *NMHR* 42 (1967).

Leonard, Olen E. *The Role of the Land Grant in the Social Organization and Social Processes of a Spanish-American Village in New Mexico.* Albuquerque: Calvin Horn, 1970. (See appendix for Spanish documents pertaining to the San Miguel grant.)

Leopold, Aldo. *A Sand County Almanac.* New York: Oxford University Press, 1968.

Loomis, Charles P. "El Cerrito, N.M." *NMHR* 33 (1958).

Magoffin, Susan Shelby. *Down the Santa Fe Trail and into Mexico.* Ed. Stella M. Drumm. New Haven, Conn.: Yale University Press, 1962.

Marquez, Angelina V. "San Miguel del Vado: The Marquez Family Tree." Typescript, Colorado College, New Mexico State Records Center, 1973.

McCall, George Archibald. *New Mexico in 1850: A Military View.* Norman: University of Oklahoma Press, 1968.

Meyer, Marian. *Mary Donoho: New First Lady of the Santa Fe Trail.* Santa Fe: Ancient City Press, 1991.

Mills, T. B. "New Mexico: San Miguel County, Illustrated Pamphlet Prepared for the World Exposition in New Orleans, 1884–1885." Las Vegas, N.M.: Carruth, 1885. New Mexico History Library.

Mocho, Jill. *Murder and Justice in Frontier New Mexico, 1821–1846.* Albuquerque: University of New Mexico Press, 1997.

Newman, Cathy. "The Pecos: River of Hard-Won Dreams." *National Geographic* (September 1993).

New Mexico Historical Sites. Santa Fe: State Planning Office, 1967.

New Mexico State Department of Welfare. Rural Council Study. "Villanueva." Typescript, Santa Fe, 1937. Donnelly Library, New Mexico Highlands University, Las Vegas, N.M.

Nostrand, Richard L. *The Hispano Homeland.* Norman: University of Oklahoma Press, 1992.

Olguin, J. P. "Where Does Justified Resentment Begin?" *New Mexico Business* 18, no. 7 (July 1967).

Oliva, Leo E. *Soldiers on the Santa Fe Trail.* Norman: University of Oklahoma Press, 1967.

Ortiz, Henry. "Legends of the Upper Pecos Valley." Typescript, 1988. Private collection of H. Ortiz, Ribera, N.M.

Perrigo, Lynn. *Gateway to Glorieta.* Boulder: Pruett, 1982.

Peters, Erich. "The Villages of the San Miguel del Vado Land Grant: An Economic and Social History of Sheep Raising in New Mexico." Typescript, Colorado College, New Mexico State Records Center, 1973.

Reeve, Frank B. *History of New Mexico.* New York: Lewis, 1961.

Ritch, W. G. *The New Mexico Bluebook.* 1883. Albuquerque: University of New Mexico Press, 1968.

Rittenhouse, Jack A. *The Santa Fe Trail: A Historical Bibliography.* Albuquerque: University of New Mexico Press, 1971.

Rock, Michael J. "The Change in Tenure New Mexico Supreme Court Decisions Have Effected upon the Common Land of Common Land Grants in New Mexico." *Social Science Journal* 13, no. 3 (October 1976).

Rosenbaum, Robert J. *Mexicano Resistance in the Southwest.* Austin: University of
Texas Press, 1981.

Ross, Spenser. "Two Villages on the Pecos." *New Mexico Magazine* 49 (spring
1971).

Roybal, David. "Santa Fe's Wild Days." *Santa Fe New Mexican,* November 15,
1996.

Salazar, David. "Las Gorras Blancas." Typescript, Carnegie Library, Las Vegas,
N.M., n.d.

Salpointe, Rev. J. B. *Soldiers of the Cross: Ecclesiastical History of New Mexico, Arizona, and Colorado.* Albuquerque: Calvin Horn, 1967.

Santa Fe New Mexican. March 20, 1864. (Article discussing death of Thomas
Rowland six years earlier.)

Scott, Wayne S. "Spanish Land Grant Problems Were Here before the Anglos."
New Mexico Business 18, no. 7 (1967).

Simmons, Marc. "Texans in New Mexico." *Santa Fe Reporter,* May 17–23, 1995.

Springer, Frank. "Land Titles in New Mexico." Address to the New Mexico Bar
Association. *Santa Fe New Mexican,* January 7, 1890.

Stoller, Marianne. "Three Church Inventories from Hispanic Frontier Communities." In *Hispanic Arts and Ethnohistory of the Southwest,* ed. Marta Weigle,
with Claudia Larcombe and Samuel Larcombe. Santa Fe: Ancient City
Press, 1983.

Sunseri, Alvin R. *The Seeds of Discord: New Mexico in the Aftermath of the Civil
War.* Chicago: Nelson Hall, 1979.

Twitchell, Ralph. *History of the Military Occupation of the Territory of New Mexico,
1846–1851.* Denver: Smith-Brooks, 1909.

———. *The Leading Facts of New Mexico History.* Cedar Rapids, Iowa: Torch
Press, 1911.

———. *The Spanish Archives of New Mexico.* 2 vols. 1914. New York: Arno, 1976.

Tyler, Daniel. "Anglo-American Penetration of the Southwest: The View from
New Mexico." *Southwestern History Quarterly* 75 (January 1972).

U.S. Bureau of the Census. 1850, 1940, 1970, 1990.

Van Ness, John R. "Spanish American vs. Anglo-American Land Tenure and
the Study of Economic Change in New Mexico." *Social Science Journal* 13
(October 1976).

Van Ness, John R., and Christine Van Ness, eds. *Spanish American Land Grants in New Mexico and Colorado.* Manhattan, Kans.: Sunflower Press, 1980.

Vigil, Maurilio. *Hispanics of New Mexico* Bristol, Ind.: Wyndham Hall, 1985.

Vigil, Tomás. "Activists Fight for Rights." *La Herencia del Norte* 10 (summer 1996).

Warren, Nancy Hunter. *Villages of Hispanic New Mexico.* Santa Fe: School of American Research, 1987.

Webb, James Josiah. *Adventures in the Santa Fe Trade, 1844–1847.* Vol. 1 in Southwest History Series. Ed. Ralph Bieber. Glendale, Calif.: Arthur Clark, 1931.

Weber, David J. "John Roland." In *Mountain Men,* ed. Leroy Hafen. Lincoln: University of Nebraska Press, 1983.

Westphall, Victor. *Mercedes Reales.* New Mexico Land Grant Series. Albuquerque: University of New Mexico Press, 1983.

White, Koch, Kelly, and McCarthy, P.A. *Land Title Study.* Santa Fe: State Planning Office, 1971.

Whitney, Virginia K., and Josephine Koogler. *Women in Education: New Mexico.* Self-published, 1977.

Williams, Jerry, and Paul McAllister, eds. *New Mexico in Maps.* Albuquerque: University of New Mexico Technical Applications Center, 1974.

Works Progress Administration. Reports by Lester Raines. Typescript, August and June 1936. San Miguel del Vado File, New Mexico History Library.